Developing Library Leaders:

A How-To-Do-It Manual® for Coaching, Team Building, and Mentoring Library Staff

Robert D. Stueart
and
Maureen Sullivan

HOW-TO-DO-IT MANUALS®

NUMBER 172

Neal-Schuman Publishers, Inc.
New York   London

Published by Neal-Schuman Publishers, Inc.
100 William St., Suite 2004
New York, NY 10038

Printed and bound in the United States of America.

The paper used in this publication meets the minimum requirements of American National Standard for Information Sciences—Permanence of Paper for Printed Library Materials, ANSI Z39.48-1992.

Library of Congress Cataloging-in-Publication Data

Stueart, Robert D.
      Developing library leaders : a how-to-do-it manual for coaching, team building, and mentoring library staff / Robert D. Stueart and Maureen Sullivan.
          p. cm. — (How-to-do-it manuals ; no. 172)
      Includes bibliographical references and index.
      ISBN 978-1-55570-725-5 (alk. paper)
      1. Library personnel management—Handbooks, manuals, etc. 2. Leadership—Handbooks, manuals, etc. I. Sullivan, Maureen. II. Title.

Z682.S89 2010
023'.3—dc22
                                                                    2010014097

To Marlies and Jack
For their faith, love, and encouragement

Contents

Foreword

The rhetoric of librarianship has been dominated in the past decade by debates about the nature and content of leadership. The collective wringing of our professional hands over the desperate need for succession planning, over the mandate for a more entrepreneurial commitment and capacity, over the mantra of "everyone a leader," and over the risks to relevance and even survival has produced a constant and sometimes blathering debate about the "nature or nurture" qualities of leadership. Who has not been confronted at a job interview with the question "What is leadership"? Which regular reader of library literature has not been overwhelmed by testimonials about various leadership development techniques inappropriately drawn from the management literature? Which professional conference attendee has not felt frustrated by the poverty of practical discussions about leadership roles, responsibilities, and techniques?

We need to focus leadership development on primal innovation, that is, creativity as a primary and fundamental component of our organizational and professional DNA. We need new approaches to radical collaboration across our local and professional communities, a commitment to more sweeping and energetic co-investments and less focus on kumbaya-like strategies. We need to deconstruct the axioms and rules of our profession and bring new coherence to the concepts and substance of libraries. Kahlil Gibran tells us that "progress lies not in enhancing what is, but in advancing toward what will be."

We need to embrace our traditional roles as libraries in new contexts. Whatever the format and tools of information services, we will remain focused on information selection, acquisition, synthesis, navigation, dissemination, interpretation, understanding, use, application, and preservation. This is a monumental set of responsibilities, enhanced and complicated by ubiquitous computing, networks, and digital content. We also see rapidly expanding tasks, as consumers, aggregators, publishers, educators, research and development organizations, entrepreneurs, and policy advocates. Does our professional leadership capacity support an expanding vision of the library as legacy, as infrastructure, as repository, as gateway, as enterprise, and as public interest?

Leadership development links with rigorous expectations for the information professional. We seek individuals who bring to the organization a wide range of subject, service, and technical expertise. This is necessary but insufficient. Across the organization, we demand a commitment to rigor, to innovation, and to assessment. We need individuals with outstanding communication, marketing, project development, and management skills. We must develop staff who are ready for political engagement, have entrepreneurial spirit, are committed to new resource development, and have an inspirational capacity. Leadership needs to be detached from charisma, as our focus must be more on substance and impact and less on superficial marketing. Marshall McLuhan once noted, "Our age of anxiety is, in great part, the result of trying to do today's jobs with yesterday's tools."

Robert Stueart and Maureen Sullivan have recognized the need in the library field, across all types of libraries and all levels of staff, for new approaches and tools for library development. The ability of libraries to expand benefit and impact, to advance community objectives, and to serve users effectively will be increasingly governed by the ability to recruit and nurture outstanding staff. And this means heightened capacity for building dynamic organizations with supportive cultures and resourceful leadership. Stueart and Sullivan have achieved an effective balance between a thoughtful context from the relevant literature and a set of tools that can be used in any library to develop understanding and skills in the areas of coaching, team building, project management, and mentoring. These are the fundamental building blocks of a healthy learning and guiding organization, that is, a successful library.

James G. Neal
Vice President for Information Services and University Librarian
Columbia University
New York, NY

Preface

Success is not counted by how high you have climbed but how many people you brought with you.

— Will Rose

The adage that "leaders are born not made" has existed for generations. Another popular myth holds that leaders are only those "isolated heroes at the top of their organization."

It is now commonly accepted that leadership is an acquired competence that can be developed. It is obvious that no single manager or administrator acts as *the* leader in any organization; rather, all of the "interdependent teams at different levels need leaders."[1] Challenging the concept of the single heroic leader is the growing number of people who have reached, or are on their way to reaching, the pinnacle of their work lives through determination and commitment to learning the "trade" by observing and doing. How can leaders be developed? We know that certain skills can be taught and learned. At the same time, there is the personal component of leadership, having a basic aptitude and will to lead and knowing that the behavior associated with that leadership is important. People who aspire to leadership positions can learn from experienced leaders.

In this context, *Developing Library Leaders: A How-To-Do-It Manual for Coaching, Team Building, and Mentoring Library Staff* is specifically aimed at organizations and individuals who seek to prepare the next generation of leaders in the information services arena, whether that development happens through in-house staff training initiatives, workshops, or additional educational programs.

What Is Leadership Development?

Unfortunately, "leadership development" has become a vogue term for staff recruitment, utilization, evaluation, and development. We use it here to focus on preparing the library's or other information organization's most valuable asset—its staff—to meet future service objectives. In an ideal setting, every information services organization should be considering a more formalized process of leadership development. In both selecting new staff and evaluating current ones, some initiative in developing potential leaders should be a priority. Information services organizations are being challenged to be accountable in their service provisions today and in their future direction. Only through effective leadership development can these goals be best achieved.

Previously, many information services organizations relied on longevity rather than on performance as a guide for advancement. But that "Peter Principle" approach is no longer relevant. Several processes are proving to be more relevant and useful in that leadership objective, including, for example, the ones emphasized in this manual: mentoring, coaching, and team building. We focus on these processes because they have the potential to increase staff job satisfaction, self-esteem, self-confidence, and motivation while simultaneously developing the next generation of leaders. Anticipating effective human resources utilization by identifying potential leaders and providing opportunities for leadership development are paramount to organizational success, encouraging individuals to grow in the organizational setting.

Leadership, both in a formal position sense and in its simplest definition, is demonstrated by "someone who has followers."[2] Leaders engage and inspire others to achieve their best. Leadership, at all levels in information services organizations, is a key to the success of the organization. Among other things, leaders are required who can inspire and develop others. This aspect of leadership requires some understanding of the importance of interplay among colleagues, a perception of the interconnectedness of personal and organizational values that lead to fulfillment of collective aspirations of the individual and the organization. This is achieved by helping others think and act beyond prevailing definitions. To effect change in the organization, responsible colleagues must encourage, cultivate, communicate, and raise self-awareness of others to enrich the organizational culture and the individual's potential.

Change is a key concept in forward-thinking information services organizations today. In the change process, it is vital to think in terms of leading people through a transition.[3] Among the most important factors of leadership in information services organizations today are the qualities of mentoring, coaching, and team building. The dynamic vision of information services requires a cadre of colleagues committed to information services as an important component in today's society. The image of a committed group of colleagues, anxious to serve the information needs of their constituency, is vital to the success of information services organizations.

How Leadership Development Has Evolved

In the past, individuals in leadership positions in the information services professions tried their utmost to "educate" potential junior members by informally developing their talents and attitudes. They believed that this type of informal mentoring was the most effective way of advancing the profession and would generate recognition, by the general public, of the important role that organized information services could play in the twenty-first century. This informal mentoring was, in many ways, exclusive and relied on what might be viewed as "chemistry" between the mentor and the protégé.

Such informal mentoring was, at that point, primarily male dominated and highly successful. To use a sage as an example, Ralph Ellsworth, Director of the University of Colorado Libraries in the 1960s and 1970s, was good at not only setting an example but also "instructing" those whom he considered potential managers—in his case, directors of university libraries. To chronicle his success, one need only consider the large number of future Association of Research Libraries (ARL) directors who benefited from his example and advice. They went on to become directors of the National Library of Agriculture as well as directors of university libraries at Michigan (Ann Arbor), California (Berkeley), North Carolina (Chapel Hill), Iowa (Iowa City), and North Texas State (Denton), among others. In a festschrift,[4] Ellsworth's gentle and sometimes not so gentle persuasion is noted to have been performed as an "effective leader, able administrator, enlightened teacher, early pioneer, dedicated advocate, and wise counselor."[5] In Ellsworth's own words, "We are like mountain climbers in unexplored territory, who, at great cost, gain one peak, only to discover that it is merely a shoulder to another, distant, higher, and more formidable range."[6]

Purpose and Organization

The purpose of *Developing Library Leaders* is to present key leadership development approaches and to encourage library and information services organizations to implement developmental processes that are necessary to prepare the next generation of information services leaders. It is a basic how-to guide for developing libraries' and information centers' most vital resources—their staff. The discussion is set in the context of human resources management issues—mentoring, coaching, team building, and succession management.

Chapters 1 and 2 provide key background information on leadership and the leader's roles and responsibilities. Each of the next chapters covers one of six key strategies for developing leaders: influence and persuasion; building and leading groups and teams; project management; coaching; mentoring; and succession planning. The book closes with a brief afterword, putting the six strategies into context.

Each chapter presents both the theoretical aspects of the strategy and ways to implement it within an organizational structure. Guidelines, examples, techniques, and other action-oriented aspects are interspersed throughout, including examples or tests on how one improves in effectiveness as a leader or how to empower others in an organization. References are made to both the library and the general management literature, as appropriate.

The techniques put forth in *Developing Library Leaders* are designed to help leaders, potential leaders, and followers to understand basic concepts and implement processes necessary for developing tomorrow's leaders. This can be most successfully achieved by first identifying the necessary components for organizational leadership and then implementing processes to ensure successful outcomes. The future leadership of our profession depends on how well each of us does this today.

Notes

1. Senge, Peter M. 1997. "Communities of Leaders and Learners." *Harvard Business Review* 75 (September–October): 32.
2. Drucker, Peter. "The Leader of the Future." New York: Drucker Foundation. *Forward*. Available: www.pfdf.org/about/index.html (accessed February 2, 2010).
3. Ferguson, Chris. "Whose Vision? Whose Values? On Leading Information Services in an Era of Persistent Change." Washington, DC: Council on Library and Information Resources. Available: www.clir.org/pubs/reports/pub123/ferguson.html (accessed February 2, 2010).
4. Stueart, Robert, ed. 1982. *Academic Librarianship: Yesterday, Today, and Tomorrow*. New York: Neal-Schuman.
5. Senge, "Communities of Leaders and Learners."
6. Stueart, *Academic Librarianship*.

Leadership for Today's Libraries and Information Services Organizations: Essential Background and Key Models

> Leadership has to take place every day. It cannot be the responsibility of the few, a rare event, or a once-in-a-lifetime opportunity.
> — Ronald A. Heifetz and Donald L. Laurie[1]

Challenges and Opportunities

In organizational and institutional settings, including libraries and other information services organizations, the terms "managing" and "leading" are often used interchangeably, sometimes misunderstood, and frequently misused or ill defined. While they are clearly related, they are not exactly the same. Still, the words "manager" and "leader" are both used to describe a person's position or responsibilities within an organization, not what he or she actually does.

One can only manage "things." Leading, on the other hand, is about people and the delicate process of influencing others to achieve mutually agreed on purposes for the greater good of the organization. One might distinguish the difference by observing that, in general, a leader is viewed as one who takes control of situations, while a manager learns to live with the situation with which he or she is presented. Further distinction would recognize that "leaders create vision and strategy while managers implement the outcome; leaders cope with change while managers cope with complexity, and leaders focus upon interpersonal aspects of the jobs, whereas managers deal with administrative duties."[2] A leader, then, is a person who influences others in an identified situation or group to obtain a particular result that will benefit the organization. Such a position does not depend on a title or on some recognition of formal authority.

More and more in today's information-intensive organizations "leaders," both those who are in official leadership positions as well as those who are unofficially engaged in leadership by opportunity taken, are involved in the career development activities of others to improve both organizations and individuals. For those who hold the

Developing Library Leaders

Think About It
Identify a leader who has influenced you. What did that person do, and how did that affect you?

formal positions of manager and administrator, the term "managerial leader" is appropriate to recognize the joint responsibilities to manage and to lead.

This all-inclusive, though somewhat elusive, motivational function, labeled "leading," focuses primarily on many of the human elements inherent within organizations. Some of these human elements, it can easily be observed, are subtle and are often invisible at first glance. This is not a recent dilemma, for, throughout history, no one single model of a successful leader has been postulated, because leaders have historically differed among the various cultures and historical periods. However, it can be postulated, probably without too much disagreement, that all authentic leaders, through their actions, appearance, and articulated values, have been able to present a vision that others might seek to emulate. Throughout history, such leaders have had "the ability to influence others in a desired direction and thus [are] able to determine the extent to which both individuals and the organization as a whole reach their goals."[3] This "vision" is accepted and adopted by followers because of its supportive nature, which, among other things, recognizes the needs and well being of a group, whether in a formal established setting or in a more informal one. Striving together, the group is energized to accomplish a vision.

In the mid-twentieth century, several theories of leadership began to emerge and influence organizations' approaches to "managing and leading." One expert encouraged organizations to take a less hierarchical, more democratic and adaptive approach.[4] His research revealed that hierarchical and autocratic approaches were good ways for teams to carry out simple tasks; however, democratic and collaborative approaches were the best ways for teams to carry out complex tasks.

Warren Bennis and Joan Goldsmith[5] offer a comprehensive definition of leadership:

Think About It
Reread this definition of leadership to identify the words and phrases that most resonate for you. Reflect upon "why?"

> Truly successful leadership today requires teams, collaboration, diversity, innovation, and cooperation. Leadership has begun to take on a new dimension. The leadership we are seeking is one that is empowering, supportive, visionary, problem-solving, creative, and shared. We are calling for a *continuum* of leadership that includes indirect leadership exerted through support and networking or scholarly studies or symbolic communication; and that extends to direct leadership of the sort that is exercised by world leaders through speeches and similar means. On that continuum, each of us can find a place and a means of expressing ourselves.

Among today's successful information services organizations, more and more attention is being paid to the most important element of leadership, that being the empowerment of team members to focus on the successful achievement of the organization's goals. All good leaders work with teams. The greatest challenge, then, lies in visioning a future of continuous, common commitment to success of the organization's goals. This can be accomplished only through the development of an enlightened and committed staff of colleagues. It requires particular attention toward a participative approach to goal setting and decision making. Activities that promote a revitalized type of commitment to these factors are making the greatest impact on innovative information services organizations. In this renewal, the designated leaders, as based on their placement on an organizational chart, are no longer perceived as "isolated heroes commanding their organizations from on high."[6] Leadership that articulates and influences the future of an organization through action requires cooperation and collaboration. Sharing information, problem solving, project planning, and enlightened performance management are all components of a more "sharing approach" to leadership in today's successful information services organizations. It requires envisioning, articulating, and influencing a future through development of a vision, culture, and set of values within the organization.

Partnerships with Staff

That libraries and other information services organizations implement methods to develop, motivate, engage, and empower staff is now considered paramount to successfully achieving organizational goals and enhancing a professional image. Leaders must have the ability to work with others to develop the organization's vision and accomplish its mission and goals and the determination to create and maintain an inclusive workplace that, through mentoring, facilitating teamwork, and resolving conflicts, fosters the development of others. An effective needs assessment is likely to identify areas for knowledge and skills development for professional staff members. The very act of empowering staff helps ensure that they are a vital part of the whole. This is one important aspect of creating a supportive environment in which knowledge and skills can be enhanced and further developed. Research has shown that professionals often leave an organization because of poor relationships with managers, lack of motivation and encouragement, and a sense of not being valued.[7]

However, "sharing" leadership is not a new idea, as anyone who has studied the management literature is well aware. The concept of participative management has been around for many years and has been dramatically detailed in previous research into "situational leadership," where the styles of directing, coaching, delegating, and supporting have been examined.[8] The concept of "situational leadership" acknowledges the different styles of leadership and the leader's ability to select the most appropriate for the situation at hand. Likewise, the "nine-nine" model of leadership in a managerial grid—which recognizes that the leader has limited control over the environment and how it impacts the task and the group—developed from the belief that management exists to encourage efficiency and performance, creativity, experimentation, and innovation and that managers learn from colleagues.[9] This was the initial model to show the importance of the team and the need for a collaborative approach.

Did You Know?
Research on what motivates people at work, including those who work in libraries, consistently shows that "participation in planning and decision making that affects me" is a key factor.

RECOMMENDED RESOURCE

Somerville, Mary M. 2009. *Working Together: Collaborative Information Practices for Organizational Learning*, for ACRL (available from the American Library Association's online store at **www.alastore.ala.org/detail.aspx?ID=2796**).

LIBRARY LEADERSHIP NETWORK LEADERSHIP DEVELOPMENT:
YOUR LIBRARY AS THE LABORATORY

Maureen Sullivan wrote the following piece for the Library Leadership Network in November 2006 (now available at lln.lyrasis.org).

In the past few years, there has been a significant increase in attention to the development of leaders in librarianship. Concern about from where the next generation of leaders will come; the recognition that supervisors, managers, and administrators in libraries today need to be effective leaders; and the knowledge that leadership is both formal (by position held) and informal (by opportunity taken) are some of the reasons for this focus of attention. There are a number of national and regional programs, many sponsored by library associations that are designed to develop leaders in libraries. Is this the most effective way to go?

Research shows that the opportunity to apply what has been learned as soon as possible is one of the most effective ways to ensure retention. The research on how competent leaders develop tells us that the most effective way to develop leadership competence is through trial and error on the job. This action-learning approach requires that the learner:

- Knows the competencies for effective leadership
- Has a clear understanding of his or her current capabilities and strengths
- Clarifies the areas for development and sets goals for development
- Makes a firm commitment to achieve the development goals
- Has ample opportunities to practice the competencies over an extended period of time, usually 6–18 months
- Has a supportive work environment
- Receives challenging assignments and carries them out under the general guidance of an experienced and competent leader/manager
- Gets regular and targeted feedback on performance
- Engages in continual self-reflection and self-awareness

Warren Bennis and Robert J. Thomas argue for what they call "crucible experiences"—complex, difficult, and challenging projects or work assignments that put individuals in situations in which they will experience deep learning and develop skills and abilities for effective leadership ("Crucibles of Leadership," *Harvard Business Review*, September 2002, p. 40). Among the frequently cited competencies for leadership are the ability to practice systems thinking—to see the big picture and to understand the dynamics and interdependencies in a situation; building relationships based on trust with many diverse individuals; managing differences and conflict situations; inspiring and influencing others to achieve results; self-awareness and effective self-management; conveying empathy and compassion toward others; acting as a change catalyst; collaborating with others and actively fostering collaboration; demonstrating a service orientation; having self-confidence; focusing attention on what matters; dealing with ambiguity; political savvy; and leading with vision and purpose.

The key competency that runs across this extensive set is the ability to establish, maintain, and nourish a complex set of relationships with others. Libraries today offer this complex set of relationships, in the context of ever-changing service expectations and work responsibilities. Libraries today are the crucible experience that Bennis describes.

Libraries, therefore, are laboratories for leadership development. What can senior executives, those who have primary responsibility for leadership development in their own organizations, do to capitalize on this opportunity?

(Continued)

LIBRARY LEADERSHIP NETWORK LEADERSHIP DEVELOPMENT:
YOUR LIBRARY AS THE LABORATORY (Continued)

The following set of Practices for Leadership Development in Your Library provide a good summary for day-to-day leadership:

- Focus on leadership development as a key initiative within the library. Make it a clear priority.
- Connect and align the leadership development program with the larger change initiatives in the library.
- Take a broad view of who will have the ability to lead. Be careful not to prejudge potential too early.
- Create opportunities for potential leaders to interact with effective, more experienced leaders.
- Identify meaningful and challenging projects and assignments that will challenge and stretch potential leaders.
- Ensure that the current formal leaders in the library are held accountable for effective leadership. Insist that their leadership practice matches the espoused leadership philosophy and values of the library.
- Make the process as transparent as possible.
- Recognize the different stages in leadership development. Warren Bennis offers one model in his article, "The Seven Ages of the Leader" (*Harvard Business Review*, January 2004, pp. 46–53).
- Remain alert to complex and challenging situations. Put managers and potential leaders in those situations.
- Make your leadership development program one that is based upon an action learning model.
- Establish a mentoring program.
- Expect current leaders to take an active role. Noel Tichy and Patricia Stacey, in their book *The Leadership Engine* (New York: HarperCollins, 1997), formulated what they call the "Teachable Point of View" approach. This approach asks leaders to do two things:
  - develop their own teachable point of view, i.e., their view of what it takes to be successful in their organization and what it takes to lead others; and
  - create a dynamic story to convey this.
- Create a learning culture within the library.

In closing, I urge you to take advantage of the "crucible": the library laboratory available to you as you do the important work of developing the leaders of tomorrow. Good luck, and be sure to share your experiences with the Library Leadership Network community!

Key Theories and Models with Application to Information Services

Previously developed leadership theories and models have become primary focal points for leadership development in the information services work environment. The early theorists, particularly those we will mention here, were attuned to "organizational culture," which encompasses patterns of behavior and subgroups within organizations. "Visioning" now plays a primary role within the leadership context, promoting the theory that the attitude of a leader can become a catalyst for change, with joint decision making and democratic leadership becoming primary foci of that approach. Among the earlier and current "gurus of culture," these are five of the most insightful models and theories discussed in library and information science courses, at national and international meetings of librarians and other information professionals, and in workshops on topics related to mentoring, coaching, and team building (which are the focus of this treatise):

1. Kouzes and Posner,[10] in *Five Practices of Exemplary Leadership*, point out that knowledge work is becoming increasingly a team-based phenomenon that is challenging traditional models of leadership. The traditional models maintain the "one person in charge" scenario, with other members as followers. Recent research and adjusted models point out that leadership can be, and often now is, shared among members of a "team." The role of leader is rotated among team members, being assigned as needed to the "lead" person who possesses the greatest key knowledge, skills, and abilities to address the specific issue facing the team at a given moment. This "just in time" approach combines both a vertical and a shared leadership stance. It tends to inspire a shared vision among colleagues and thereby promote a shared future vision of organizational success. Such a risk-taking approach also challenges the status quo methods used in more traditional organizations by fostering collaboration and empowerment that both encourages and enables shared planning and decision making. Kouzes and Posner identify five keys to success: (i) role modeling (demonstrating the way); (ii) inspiring a shared vision; (iii) challenging the process, the status quo; (iv) enabling others to act; and (v) encouraging the heart, i.e., enthusiasm in the work of the organization.

2. The need satisfaction model of motivation of Abraham Maslow[11] focuses on self-awareness, self-knowledge, and self-understanding. It is enumerated in a series of sequential stages as physiological needs; safety needs; needs for love, affection, and a sense of belonging; need for esteem; and need for self-actualization. All of these are important points to consider in information services organizations.

3. Bennis and Nanus[12] identify "transformational leaders" as those who are committed to transforming followers into self-empowered leaders and change agents through the "Four I's": (i) Idealized Influence (role model); (ii) Inspiration Motivation; (iii) Intellectual Stimulation (creativity and innovation); and (iv) Individual Consideration (i.e., mentoring). These topics are discussed in many workshops and conferences on leadership in information services. Bennis and Nanus also articulated what followers expect from leaders—trust; optimism; meaning, purpose, and direction; and a focus on results—as well as the three organizational requirements of learning: inquiry-based

---

RECOMMENDED RESOURCE

Jim Kouzes and Barry Posner's *Leadership Practices Inventory* is an effective planning and development tool used by many leaders in libraries. It is available, along with a number of supporting resources, at **www.leadershipchallenge.com**.

and reflective culture, empowerment of all involved, and alignment throughout.

4. Goleman, Boyatzis, and McKee[13] maintain that a leader's behavior is as important as other attributes, including vision and intelligence. Their research assesses leadership styles—how they are used and how they are perceived by others. The researchers identify four so-called behavioral domains: (i) Self Awareness: includes the ability to read our own emotions and recognize their impact on others, know our own limits and strengths, and have a good sense of our capabilities; (ii) Self Management: encompasses having emotional self-control; being honest, adaptable, and driven to improve performance and meet standards of excellence; and possessing initiative and optimism; (iii) Social Awareness: requires having empathy and sensitivity to others' emotions, taking an interest in others, having organizational and political awareness, and being willing to serve the needs of both customers and employees; and (iv) Relationship Management: rests on the abilities to guide and motivate others, influence people and help them develop, serve as a catalyst for change, manage conflict, and forge the bonds required for effective teamwork and collaboration.

5. Bolman and Deal's[14] "Four Frames" is a four-frame model with which to understand organizations and leadership within organizations. The frames are the lenses through which people see the world and place that world into order. The researchers maintain that every person has a personal and preferred "frame" through which they gather information and make judgments that determine their behavior. They classify the frames into four categories: (i) the Structural, wherein the manager tries to develop and maintain a "structure" that is appropriate to the issue at hand—a structural hierarchical approach; (ii) the Human Resources approach, wherein the manager attempts to be responsive to needs and goals to gain commitment and loyalty—a more collegial approach; (iii) the Political approach, wherein the manager focuses on understanding the political reality of organizations, including the conflicts and competition that develop in them, and employs networking, coalition building, and bargaining to build support; and (iv) the Symbolic, where a shared vision and values allows for the leader to be a catalyst of both decisions and actions.

> **RECOMMENDED RESOURCE**
>
> Lee G. Bolman and Terrence E. Deal, *Reframing Organizations: The Leadership Kaleidoscope*. Available: **www.tnellen.com/ted/tc/bolman.html**.

As is evident, many theories have evolved in the past 50 years to suggest what makes a leader successful. Not one of the theories adequately explains leadership; however, they do help identify and explain many of the variables that contribute to being a successful leader. When one evaluates the characteristics of leaders, as many studies have done, it becomes clear that some traits and talents are inherent whereas others are learned. Among the most important of the latter, at least from an organizational standpoint, are mentoring, team building, coaching, talent development, and succession planning—all now becoming more recognized as vital components of leadership development. For too long, these concepts and traits have been at best misunderstood and at worst simply ignored. One primary reason is that some of these noninherent characteristics cannot be exclusively taught but rather must also be effectively learned in the workplace and other information-based settings. However, in many of today's information services organizations, where a data-rich but information-poor climate continues to predominate, one primary goal is to attract, enlighten, retain, and further encourage talented staff, both professional and support. Every future-oriented information services organization strives to keep talented, innovative members and is continuously seeking ways to strengthen its team and develop succession planning activities.

The primary issue, then, becomes one of recognizing and supporting talented staff who have the potential of being tomorrow's leaders. How does an organization first identify and then actively support these individuals? How does an organization that is focused primarily on hiring and training staff begin to address the unfortunate level of neglect in fostering those with potential leadership qualities? Fortunately, this component is now becoming more recognized and promoted as an essential ingredient in the continuing value and success of an information services organization.

Other important issues must be addressed as well if the organization is to remain relevant. Healthy morale among focused employees does not happen without effort. A positive outcome requires foresight and planning and involves the commitment of all units within the organization. Such a "bottom-to-top" approach, leaving no talented employee behind, enables an organization to develop and maintain qualified, committed personnel through a pro-systemwide active program of both development and promotion of staff, as well as recruitment of qualified potential staffers. This approach empowers an innovative organization to develop and maintain a success-oriented reputation by continuously strengthening its workforce while developing future leaders of the profession. An organization is not likely to manage this if it does not know who its people really are and what individual members' potentials might be. Actively supporting staff development, recognizing talents, and maintaining a succession planning orientation are all components in the process of identifying and preparing suitable employees through mentoring, coaching, and team building.

Engaging and Motivating Staff for High Performance

Fortunately some information services organizations today are following a holistic, team-based approach to leadership by empowering individuals to make decisions about their work and to resolve issues at lower levels in the organization. Such encouraging actions demonstrate confidence and motivate colleagues toward greater efforts. When those empowered staff feel a greater part of the solution, they are more likely to buy in to the organization's mission and contribute more enthusiastically to its success.

In today's knowledge-based society, an information services organization's most important asset is the energy and loyalty of its people—the intellectual capital that should be motivated and forward thinking. Yet one of the biggest issues, in general, in such organizations remains that of underestimating the value and potential of talented, knowledgeable people instead of recognizing and challenging them.

Staff motivation and development, in a future-focused information services environment, requires a cooperative, comprehensive, continuing effort between management and individuals with talent to recognize and promote the talents of future leaders. The primary question remains one of "How can an organization best achieve this?" Of course, any such future-directed program must first seek to identify an individual's potential for development. This process can and should align the individual's personal goals with the overall achievement goals of the organization. Likewise, alignment of the complementary objectives can serve to enhance the identification and development of leadership talents of colleagues while at the same time promoting individual successful goal achievement within the organization. Such a strategy will both improve morale and encourage succession planning within the organization.

We know that certain skills can be taught but that other skills and attitudes are most successfully learned over a period of time through a variety of innovative activities supported by an institution that is committed to the concept of staff development through coaching, team-building, mentoring, leadership training, and succession planning. Until recently, practitioners and educators alike had focused primarily on specific techniques and skills rather than on some of those key, somewhat elusive, developmental concepts. This process has been described in the professional journal literature, in conference programming, and in the educational curricula of related higher educational programs. The traditional hierarchical, authoritarian organization, with control emanating from the top downward, now is giving way to more participative management and shared decision making in many forward-thinking and forward-acting organizations. New approaches to leadership theory and practice are advancing those factors. This developing view of human resources management is enhancing and promoting mutual respect among colleagues by using the recognized talents among the collegial pool and making a unified commitment to the organizational goals. The focus is on mission and vision rather than exclusively on tasks and duties, with both now playing an equally important, yet complementary, role in an organization's success.

In such a process, the myth that leaders are born, not made, can easily be debunked by thoughtful analysis of who current or future successful leaders are or might become and how they have achieved, are achieving, or will achieve such status. We now recognize that leadership is developed through both initiative and inspiration. The complementary talents and activities can be molded through various initiatives, primarily falling into the three "C's" categories of cooperation, collaboration, and commitment. Many of today's followers are, indeed, destined to become tomorrow's leaders. A primary focus then is on how an organization can encourage, enlighten, and effect this into a successful transition. Is there a plan for this development? If so, how is it being implemented within the organization? "From a philosophical standpoint, the approach to participative management centers on the belief that people at all levels of an organization can develop a genuine interest in its success and can do more than merely perform their assigned duties."[15]

This participative management approach involves sharing in "visioning for the organization," as well as in decision making, problem solving, project planning, and consequently in evaluating results and adjusting deficiencies that are identified in that process. Communication, innovative strategic thinking, and ethical behavior are all components of an approach that results in decision making at the primary level in an organization, at the very level where the most pertinent information can be most effectively gleaned, analyzed, and acted on to support a decision. Today most successful leaders recognize that this type of cooperation and collaboration is important within an organization. From this development, it can be anticipated that leadership in the future information center will be distributed among diverse individuals and teams who share responsibility for creating the organization's future.[16]

In today's information-intense world, it is almost impossible for any one person to successfully direct an information services organization as "the" leader without concerted help and support of others. Such teams in innovative organizations require interdependent direction and solicit support for leaders who are "team players," willing and anxious, with initiative and open minds, to join their committed associates in the success of the information services enterprise. This approach naturally presents continuous challenges and committed development of staff at every level in the organization.

It is equally important to remember that such factors as training, staff development, team building, coaching, career development, and mentoring each contains nuances of difference and require different approaches and techniques in accomplishing the overall organizational goals. At the same time, it should be recognized that they are complementary approaches for organizational success. In this general mix, each of these can be interpreted as helping to shape positions and careers that are satisfying for talented colleagues. These factors are often identified by their own initiatives or by colleagues at a more experienced level. Most successful organizations pay attention to each of these factors in supporting the successful achievement for the benefit of both individuals and organizations. Identification and encouragement are ways of retaining talented individuals and helping them achieve the type of career success for which they might aspire. It also can enable organizations to keep valuable human resources as well as prepare those individuals for leadership positions, whether in that organization or in another one. Attention to this type of planning also enables organizations to recognize the complex issues of career development in the changing environment of information services.

At the same time, even though it continues to be postulated by some that leadership is learned, not taught, it should be obvious that teaching can and must take place, balancing theory and practice in the process. Aspiring leaders need role models and guidance. Leadership development programs are now relatively common, with many organizations and institutions consciously initiating them to help new practitioners and other staff, adding practice and skills development to the theory embedded in information services. Leadership shadowing is becoming another frequent program in information services organizations where learners observe someone, critically reflect on and contemplate what they observed, and assess that person's style of work and interpersonal skills, as well as undertake a situational analysis. The following chapters discuss the most pertinent activities and approaches that ensure success in today's libraries and information services organizations.

> **Did You Know?**
> The Association of Research Libraries established its Research Library Leadership Fellows program several years ago for its member libraries to help develop the next generation of leaders (see **www.arl.org**).

Notes

1. Heifetz, Ronald A., and Donald L. Laurie. 2001. "The Work of Leadership." *Harvard Business Review* Reprint RO111K (December): 5–14. Available: itk.hbsp.harvard.edu/demos/hb_solution/content/Read/work_of_leadership.pdf (accessed February 26, 2010).
2. Isaac, Wilfred, J. Zerbe, and Douglas C. Pitt. 2001. "Leadership and Motivation: The Effective Application of Expectancy Theory." *Journal of Managerial Issues* 13 (Summer): 213.
3. Stueart, Robert D., and Barbara B. Moran. 2007. *Library and Information Center Management*, 7th ed. Westport, CT: Libraries Unlimited, p. 322.
4. Bennis, Warren. 1989. *On Becoming a Leader*. Boston: Addison Wesley.
5. Bennis, Warren and Joan Goldsmith. 2003. *Learning to Lead: A Workbook on Becoming a Leader*. New York: Basic Books, p. xv.
6. Senge, Peter M. 1997. "Communities of Leaders and Learners." *Harvard Business Review* 75 (September–October): 32.
7. Werther, William B., Jr., and Evan M. Berman. 2001. *Third Sector Management: The Art of Managing Nonprofit Organizations*. Washington, DC: Georgetown University Press.
8. Hersey, Paul, and Kenneth H. Blanchard. 1993. *Situational Leadership*. Englewood Cliffs, NJ: Prentice-Hall.
9. Blake, R.R., and J.S. Mouton Blake. 1964. *The Managerial Grid*. Houston: Gulf.
10. Kouzes, James M., and Barry Z. Posner. 2003. *The Five Practices of Exemplary Leadership*, revised. New York: Jossey-Bass.
11. Maslow, Abraham H. 1943. "A Theory of Human Motivation." *Psychological Review* 50 (July): 395.
12. Bennis, Warren, and Burt Nanus. 1986. *Leaders: The Strategies for Taking Charge*. New York: Harper & Row.
13. Goleman, Daniel, Richard E. Boyatzis, and Annie McKee. 2002. *Primal Leadership: Learning to Lead with Emotional Intelligence*. Cambridge, MA: Harvard Business Press.

14. Bolman, Lee G., and Terrence E. Deal. 2008. *Reframing Organizations*, 3rd ed. New York: Jossey-Bass Management Series.
15. Conner, Daryl R. 1993. *Managing at the Speed of Change: How Resilient Managers Succeed and Prosper Where Others Fail*. New York: Villard, p. 198.
16. Senge, Peter. 1997. "Communities of Leaders and Learners." *Harvard Business Review* 75 (September–October): 32.

The Leader's Role and Responsibilities

> If your actions inspire others to dream more, learn more, do more and become more, you are a leader.
>
> — John Quincy Adams

Key Competencies for Effective Leadership

Leadership is a multifaceted, fascinating topic. However, at its most basic level, one can describe it as the ability to inspire confidence and support among followers that permits the group to fulfill the unit's mission. "Influence," "vision," "mission," and "goals" are terms that are usually included in its broader definition. One thing we know that distinguishes successful organizations is that they are directed by dynamic and effective leaders. An important lesson that successful leaders learn early is that no one can lead alone. By simple definition, leaders do not operate in isolation. Instead, leadership always depends on cooperation and collaboration. It is also becoming accepted, in today's world, that leadership is a quality that can be developed. Leadership is an acquired competency that is the result of many circumstances. Therefore, in today's successful information services organizations a more participative leadership atmosphere is emerging, one that is not only encouraged but is being demanded.

This vitalized post-heroic leadership approach is evident when decisions are shared, leading to a sense of shared organizational ownership.[1] Such an approach recognizes leadership qualities and contributions among staff at all levels in an organization. This behooves effective managers and supervisors in a hierarchical organization to develop leadership skills. Likewise, leaders are required to demonstrate certain management skills in order to effectively influence colleagues. Such collaboration is becoming an important aspect of what individuals want and need in their work lives. This is most apparent in the trend toward team-based organizational development.

IN THIS CHAPTER:

- ✔ Key Competencies for Effective Leadership
- ✔ Techniques in Establishing Confidence
- ✔ Self-Assessment, Style, and Performance
- ✔ Ethical Leadership Practice and Social Responsibility
- ✔ Planning for Self-Development
- ✔ Developing Self-Confidence

Think About It
What is your personal definition of leadership? How does it fit with the traditional description of leadership?

RECOMMENDED RESOURCE

To learn more about the Library Leadership Network, a community of practice where leaders (and those who will become leaders) assemble to share best practices, discuss issues, find solutions, and build community, go to **lln.lyrasis.org**.

But what is leadership, really? Why is it so important in today's library and information services organizations? How can it be applied in those organizations? Simply defined, leadership is both formal, as indicated by position held, and informal, through opportunities taken by individuals in organizations. Leadership includes a number of competencies, the most frequently cited of which are the ability to practice systems thinking—to see the big picture and to understand the dynamics and interdependencies in a situation; build relationships based on trust with many diverse individuals; manage differences and conflict situations; inspire and influence others to achieve results; be self-aware, have self-confidence, and practice effective self-management; convey empathy and compassion toward others; act as a change catalyst; collaborate with others and actively foster collaboration; demonstrate a service orientation; focus attention on what matters; deal with ambiguity; demonstrate political savvy; and lead with vision and purpose. A tall order to ponder and address. One source of discussions about successful endeavors and challenges is the Library Leadership Network.[2]

There is much discussion but no solid consensus on what leadership qualities an individual must ultimately possess. However, there is some general agreement that among the most important characteristics of a leader are those embodied in the "Three E's Qualities" of Encourage, Empower, and Energize. These attributes, whether singly or collectively, allow a leader to ultimately develop a shared vision of what is most important and ultimately possible.

In such a collective effort, to use a cliché, a leader "does the right thing," whereas a more passive manager's reaction would be to "do things right.[3] A leader is not always the person who holds the formal leadership position or even one who, because of status, some assume is the leader. Rather, a leader is anyone persuasive enough to effect positive change within an organization. Leaders influence others in accomplishing goals for the organization by simply and effectively applying their leadership attributes, including beliefs, values, ethics, character, knowledge, and skills, to the issue at hand. They employ their own inner self to things they know and/or can do to accomplish objectives and directions for organizational development in ways that make it more cohesive and coherent. They employ their *beliefs*, the assumptions and convictions that they hold to be evident; their values, by which they determine the importance of various alternatives; their ethics, or standards of acceptable behavior; and their character, including such attributes as energy, determination, self-discipline, and willpower. When these are supplemented with innate *knowledge* (i.e., experience, contextual information, values, and expert insight), which provides a framework for evaluating and incorporating new experiences and information), and *skills* (i.e., expertise developed in the course of both training and experience),[4] then leadership is delegated to those individuals and teams who are ultimately responsible for creating the organizations' futures. A leader in these instances is challenged first to create a vision that inspires others and second to execute that vision successfully, with the help of followers. The goals, priorities, values, and other motivating attributes set the stage for organizational success, while at the same time recognizing that various other social, economic, technological, administrative, and organizational factors exist and affect ultimate success.

Additionally, as a side benefit, a concerted, in-depth analysis of the organization aids in developing a marketing strategy to promote the information services organization within its political, economic, social, and technological environment.[5] Addressing the success of those marketing efforts ultimately facilitates a coalition of external support and effective broad-based communication, thereby ameliorating resistance to change and facilitating the implementation of successful change actions. The effectiveness of such efforts must be measured through the development of a scale of success to maintain a balance between continuity and change. This requires the development of measurements of the success of the organization toward accomplishing those identified goals.

Leaders are ultimately identified by who they are, their character and beliefs, what they know, their knowledge of human nature and their experiences, as well as what they do, through motivation and direction, to empower others. One vital competency is the ability to establish, maintain, and nourish a complex set of relationships with others—staff members, higher administrators in the organization, patrons, funding authorities, etc. These various constituencies each requires development of a culture of trust, integrity, risk taking, and creative thinking. Information services organizations, which include these groups, are prime venues for developing and maintaining effective and efficient leaders. But, how is someone's leadership potential first identified and then encouraged? Some areas of competency are easily demonstrated by effective leaders.[6] They are universal in application and have been recognized as important in the process of leadership development. Among the attributes and applications is behavior that is consistent with the espoused values and culture of the organization. Leaders are charged with that integrity.

One of the most important functions of a leader is to develop and structure the organization based on its strategic goals, most of which are evident in its strategic plans. Leaders will initiate, identify, and develop strategies based on internal and external opportunities to achieve the organization's vision, mission, and broad goals.[7] Several necessary competencies include the art of visioning and the ability to employ change management concepts toward what some researchers call "transformational leadership." These important management traits are becoming expected of leaders in today's information services organizations. These guiding principles, and adherence to them, can encourage members of an information services organization to identify and pursue common goals and give members a sense of control, while fostering creative thinking.

Some of these factors offer suggestions of processes, methods, and systems applicable for library and information services organization.[8]

Such forward-thinking initiatives can both enable and enhance the development of future plans and actions based on an ever-changing organization that is adept at adjusting to requirements in the greater external environment. Leaders are expected to be strategic and creative problem solvers. Such effort involves, first, a systematic approach on the part of leaders toward identifying a "corporate" knowledge base that demonstrates the various competencies and skills necessary to accomplish organizational goals and then measuring the effectiveness of the organization in working toward that achievement. Information services leaders must through actions, appearance, and articulated values present a vision that others want to emulate.[9]

Effective leaders are flexible, versatile, and innovative with a social awareness. They are adept at communicating, motivating, and resolving conflicts as well as team building, mentoring, coaching, building and leading groups and teams, and succession planning. This not only enhances the organization's ultimate success but also encourages the individual through the efforts of mentoring, coaching, team building, and feedback. A useful evaluation tool to assess a leader's competencies and attitudes is the *Leadership Practices Inventory*.[10] Leaders can use this tool to evaluate their own strengths and weaknesses with the intention of correcting their weaknesses.

A leader is able to effectively communicate through oral presentations, written eloquence, active listening, and technological means to enlighten and persuade followers and other observers. Crisis management requires one of the most delicate sets of organizational skills that a leader must possess. This includes maintaining public relations as well as external relations with a wider community.

Techniques in Establishing Confidence

Leadership style and employee performance are linked to and dictated by employees' experiences in the organization. Generally, as one might expect, research has shown a higher correlation between a positive climate and increased productivity. Therefore, what a leader does and how he or she does it drives an organizational climate to be productive or, conversely, unproductive. Leaders use several techniques to develop confidence among employees and other stakeholders. These are the most important:

1. **Establishing trust**: Leaders earn and retain respect within the organization by demonstrating and employing their knowledge and skills. Trust is a vital factor, and it is most often evidenced in the actions that leaders take, or do not take, which should be consistent, even-handed, and reflect both the original commitments and an atmosphere of open dialogue and communication in design and deed. Public relations is the best tool for explaining the organization's values to colleagues and the public. Interactive media, including websites, online services,

CORE COMPETENCIES FOR LEADERS

Supervising
- Commands the trust and respect of others as one who is knowledgeable, focused, and consistent
- Creates a clear sense of purpose, mission, and key results
- Demonstrates an understanding of others' needs, motives, and personal styles

Developing Employees
- Encourages others to achieve developmental goals
- Fosters opportunities for learning and development
- Acknowledges others' work and achievements

Planning and Organizing
- Prepares efficient and effective plans
- Completes projects successfully and on time
- Uses resources effectively and efficiently to achieve goals

Motivating
- Establishes a positive, motivating team atmosphere
- Regularly provides reinforcement and rewards to staff
- Empowers others to take the initiative and make decisions

Mentoring
- Contributes to the continued growth of employees
- Acts as an advisor or positive role model
- Willingly teaches and coaches

Leading
- Recognizes and promotes the need to accept change
- Works with others to build a collaborative work environment based on trust, candor, and respect
- Actively seeks out, develops, and maintains good working relationships with staff

Resolving Conflict
- Negotiates with others to achieve workable solutions

Resolving Conflict *(Continued)*
- Mediates conflicts and finds solutions satisfactory to all parties
- Creates an environment where conflict and dialogue is well managed

Affirming Diversity in the Workplace
- Takes advantage of the creative possibilities inherent in a diverse workforce
- Takes proactive steps to increase departmental diversity and recognizes and appreciates differences in people
- Proactively minimizes barriers and ensures equality of opportunities

Evaluating
- Establishes clear, specific, realistic, and challenging goals and performance standards
- Provides regular, honest, and constructive feedback to improve performance
- Demonstrates skill, sensitivity, and confidence in conducting performance evaluations

Delegating
- Delegates challenging responsibilities to staff
- Creates a clear and easily understood approach to accomplishing work
- Effectively uses the team to solve problems, make decisions, and prepare action plans

Service Orientation
- Reaches out to be helpful, get answers, or solve problems
- Demonstrates concern for public satisfaction of constituents and customers
- Displays diplomacy and courtesy

Judgment
- Responds and acts appropriately
- Assesses consequences of actions
- Makes timely and accurate decisions

Commitment
- Displays enthusiastic and dedicated behavior
- Gets actively involved in the organization

Commitment *(Continued)*
- Is achievement oriented and reliable

Teamwork
- Builds alliances to achieve objectives
- Offers assistance and support
- Promotes cooperation and trust

Flexibility
- Actively considers new ideas
- Adapts to change
- Demonstrates a willingness to learn new skills and methods

Initiative
- Anticipates needs and takes appropriate next steps
- Originates creative ideas and methods
- Requires little or no direction and is proactive

Technical Skills
- Demonstrates proficiency in a variety of standard platforms
- Understands concepts and relationships
- Adapts to new hardware, software, upgrades, and other technological changes

Communication Skills
- Shares knowledge and information with appropriate individuals
- Provides timely and accurate information
- Listens, understands, and communicates clearly

Organizational Skills
- Prioritizes work under time constraints
- Manages multiple tasks and meets deadlines
- Streamlines procedures

Accountability
- Takes personal responsibility
- Follows through on commitments
- Implements decisions

Problem Solving
- Seeks out relevant information before making decisions
- Demonstrates persistence in overcoming obstacles

and blogs, as well as more traditional methods, are key methods of communicating with both staff and those who use the information services. Sustained trust and integrity are established among staff through open communication and continuing dialogue (orally, electronically, and in print), information dissemination, and policy initiatives. This is enhanced by both using and seeking feedback to improve organizational initiatives.

2. **Seeking feedback**: Leaders traditionally seek feedback to elicit the support of staff, elected officials, and other stakeholders to improve performance. To be successful, this effort requires the art of listening, analyzing, and responding to meaningful comments and suggestions. In addition, many organizations have in place formal processes to measure management performance. These processes are designed to discover and address both strengths and weaknesses and to serve as guidelines for developing a leader's talents. A well thought out program is also an important tool to evaluate a formal leader's performance. A formal leader must be able to communicate effectively so that goals are identified and the team effort is directed toward those goals.

3. **Developing collaboration and communication**: Effective leaders must understand and empathize with the diverse needs and agendas of staff as well as external constituencies and shareholder groups. A collegial approach to sharing information ensures that the organization can make decisions in a timely manner. This includes facilitating the professional and personal development of colleagues through formal mentoring, team building, and coaching programs.

4. **Motivating and promoting colleagues**: Motivation techniques include reward systems, performance appraisals, role clarifications, and assigning challenging responsibilities that require colleagues to learn new things. Providing opportunities for further professional and personal development helps instill confidence and build expertise. This process requires a spirit of empowerment of colleagues. Such efforts are most important in the success of organizational goals and are evidenced in such activities as mentoring, coaching, and team building.

5. **Visioning**: Leaders encourage a shared vision through imagination, insight, and boldness. This involves imagining where an organization should go but not prescribing or forcing the required efforts to arrive there. It is crucial for a successful leader to have a vision, and sharing that vision creates a sense of commonality among colleagues and gives coherence to the diverse activities that take place within the organization. The vision is one of a future reality seen now, and a leader openly shares information, thereby empowering knowledge in others.

QUICK TIP

The key to providing successful feedback is to be direct, specific, and timely when addressing someone's behavior. It also is important to check for understanding.

Did You Know?
Motivation in human services organizations is particularly challenging because managers have limited control over formal rewards such as salary and promotions. Managerial leaders must therefore use informal rewards. *1001 Rewards & Recognition Fieldbook*, by Bob Nelson and Dean Spitzer (Workman, 2003), is an excellent resource for no-cost and low-cost ideas.

Think About It
What is your vision of where your organization should be five years from now? What do you envision your work to be?

DEVELOPING BASIC LEADERSHIP TALENTS

1. *Foresight—i.e., the ability to envision the future and to think for the long term as well as the present.* Middle managers will have an important role in monitoring the external environment, identifying trends and changes that will affect the library, and making changes to internal systems to assure effective performance. The ability to anticipate changes in work and in staff needs will be important as will the ability to organize the work to allow flexibility so that changes can be made as needed.

2. *The ability to imagine new realities and share them with staff to develop a shared vision of the future.* Setting direction and helping staff to see their work and the problems they encounter as part of the larger library system is critical to the staff's ability to solve complex problems and to keep pace with change.

3. *A focus on quality service and continuous improvement.* This focus is the hallmark of Total Quality Management (TQM) programs. Some research libraries have begun to implement TQM. A number of others have started service improvement programs.

4. *An ability to project consequences of action and to assess the risks in decision making.*

5. *Actively seeking information from a variety of sources within the library, and the university community, and beyond.* Managers also will need to be skilled in assessing who needs to know what and selecting the most effective and efficient means to communicate that information.

6. *Establishing working relationships is based on trust and mutual respect.* This requires honest and open communication, consistent behavior, and a willingness to be influenced as well as to exercise influence.

7. *Persistence and perseverance* are two traits of Rosabeth Moss Kanter's "change master."

8. *An understanding of organizational values and their relationship to the core mission of the library.*

9. *Communicating values to staff so that they can see their relationship to the work performed and develop their own commitment to those values.*

10. *Behaving in ways that are congruent with personal values and the espoused values of the library.* Authentic behavior is critically important to the development of working relationships that are based on trust.

11. *A willingness to challenge behavior that is inconsistent with organizational values or norms and performance expectations.* This requires a commitment to providing honest feedback to staff that is specific and delivered in a way that conveys support for the person but also provides a clear expectation that the person will act to correct the problem.

12. *An understanding of the political environment,* both within the library and externally, and the ability to interact effectively with "key players."

13. *A willingness to share power by creating meaningful opportunities for staff involvement in problem solving, decision making, and planning.* This involvement is critical to the development of staff commitment. It is also very important to library performance because the staff doing the work usually have the best information.

14. *Nurturing the development of others.* Helping staff to solve problems by engaging them in a process in which the manager is a helper, not the problem solver, thereby encouraging staff to be accountable and to assume the responsibility for solving their own problems.

15. *Taking an active interest in the career development of staff.* Managers must see the staff member as a component of the library organization as well as the incumbent of a particular position.

16. *Identifying the special abilities and potential in each person.* Accepting others for who they are, valuing differences, and promoting diversity among the staff are important components of this.

17. *Strong self-awareness and knowledge.* Managers are role models for staff. An accurate self concept and an understanding of strengths and weaknesses are important.

(*Source:* Maureen Sullivan. 1992. "The Changing Role of the Middle Manager in Research Libraries." *Library Trends* 41, no. 2: 269–281.)

Self-Assessment, Style, and Performance

Several "C" terms describe the traits of leaders. They are Committed, Compassionate, Collaborative, Courageous, Confident, and Compromising. Although these traits have been found to be associated with what is commonly viewed as leadership, there probably is no such thing as a single leadership type or style. Nevertheless, various skills, abilities, and personalities can be identified.

In attempts to analyze and assess particular leadership styles, the traits of "telling, selling, participating, and delegating" are often mentioned and discussed. In addition, attempts to identify concepts about the personalities of leaders mention characteristics such as extravert/introvert as well as the nuances of intuition, thinking, and perceiving. It is sometimes useful for an individual/leader to try to identify his or her particular leader's style of management in order to assess how that style might impact a particular organization's challenges. Leaders will analyze their own styles when they perceive a need for change.

Whatever the style, one can surmise that a person in a leadership position is either operational in approach or more strategic, and therefore his or her leadership characteristics will reflect one or the other approach, for example, asking versus telling, supporting versus pushing, and—particularly important—empowering others versus taking charge. Researchers[11] have categorized and described some leadership "styles" that appear to be most appropriate, depending on the circumstances within an organization. Each style, as might be expected, can have varying effects upon followers. These leadership styles include the characteristics of (1) developing other leaders, (2) acting as good role models, and (3) treating people the way they, themselves, would like to be treated. Some of the most often postulated traits include the important ones of truly listening and being able to elicit and synthesize the best from group thinking by identifying good ideas and ultimately facilitating directions/decisions into actions. Forward thinking and acting, an effective leader also considers what should transpire next, thereby moving discussions and decisions forward in a positive manner, while at the same time minimizing criticism, tension, and complaints, toward a successful conclusion. This is also an important step in the process of mentoring, coaching, and team building future "leaders" within an organization. The sharing and "what next" approach instills respect and accountability for that individual among colleagues regardless of the position within the organization or personality of the holder.

Some researchers have postulated that leadership styles fall into two basic categories: (1) authoritative and (2) participative. However, it is not quite that simple. There are many variances and nuances within a basic style. Numerous studies have evaluated various leadership styles and described the strengths and weaknesses that each might bring to an organization.[12] Consider these six basic styles, listed from the most conservative to the most liberal, when you evaluate your own and other's leadership traits:

1. **Coercive**: seeks compliance from others, maintaining a rather tight control and having a more negative than positive attitude. This type of leader employs one-way communication, usually downward, rarely consulting other persons in the organization because their judgment is not valued. Coercive leaders focus on:

   a. Issuing directions without soliciting input or listening to reactions ("do as I tell you") in order to maintain tight control

   b. Maintaining tight control of employees through such forms of monitoring as frequently observing, demanding reports, and overtly criticizing

   c. Relying on negative, sometimes damaging corrective feedback and criticism about what is done wrong and needs to be corrected

   d. Employing embarrassing actions, such as name calling, fist pounding, and publicly chastising to embarrass someone into compliance

   e. Announcing negative consequences of an employee's failure to comply with instructions

2. **Authoritative**: gives "autocratic" directions to motivate staff toward a self-conceived organizational vision. This approach focuses on accomplishing tasks according to preestablished policies and procedures. Authoritative leaders focus on:

   a. Strategic management thinking and doing, requiring followers to adhere to management-stated directions

   b. Using persuasion, even threatening, tactics to gain staff acceptance of predetermined decisions

   c. Presenting his or her own vision and directions as "best" for the organization

   d. Using coercion to force acceptance and to influence employees of the identified approach, leaving little doubt of who is in charge

   e. Developing and monitoring performance according to management's own ideas

   f. Employing both positive and negative feedback to motivate

3. **Affiliative**: seeks to establish harmony and good will in the organization. Affiliative leaders focus on:

   a. Employing a "touchy-feely" approach to establish harmony and cooperation through a feel-good approach

   b. Minimizing tension among employees with intraorganizational "social activities"

   c. Placing primary attention on staff needs, with work efforts remaining secondary

   d. Avoiding, whenever possible, staff confrontations and using positive reinforcement to gain staff support

Did You Know?
Daniel Goleman and colleagues later changed the "authoritative" designation to "visionary" leadership styles (see **changingminds.org/ disciplines/leadership/styles/six_ emotional_styles.htm**).

4. **Democratic** (also called **participative**): attempts to develop group consensus on major issues and utilizes a group management approach to decision making. Democratic leaders focus on:

   a. Seeking staff input in setting organizational direction and in the follow-up activities of achieving the objectives of an organization's strategic plan

   b. Attempting to build consensus through such efforts as group decision making, thereby ensuring that all views are expressed in the decision-making processes

   c. Rewarding group performance rather than identifying individuals, thereby avoiding jealousy and dissention among staff

5. **Pace-setting**: employs, and even exaggerates, high performance standards. Pace-setting leaders focus on:

   a. Motivating high performance of both individuals and competent teams

   b. Leading with enthusiasm and with the full expectation that employees will follow

   c. Maintaining an independent stature rather than developing team leaders

   d. Delegating responsibilities to outstanding staff performers who require minimal direction

   e. Issuing explicit directions in an attempt to develop those other staff members who are not performing according to a pre-established norm

   f. Downplaying teamwork while focusing on individual employee efforts

6. **Coaching**: exerting efforts to effectively develop staff members for future performance and promotion (discussed in more detail in Chapter 6). Coaching leaders focus on:

   a. Identifying strengths and weaknesses of colleagues, with efforts to correct any identified weaknesses

   b. Developing each member's long-range goals, with potential for promotion to greater responsibilities

   c. Consulting with staff to identify and correct important work-related issues

   d. Recognizing that long long-term organizational success is paramount and that mistakes are learning experiences along the way

As mentioned, there are other leadership styles, which can generally be thought of as variations of these six. It might even be argued that these six are arbitrary divisions. For instance, where does the "laissez-faire style," with a hands-off approach and little authoritative direction, fall? Certainly this category of leader is likely to allocate decision-making responsibilities to others in the organization. And what about the "bureaucratic style," which maintains strict preset organizational policies and procedures? Other styles have nuisances of difference that are difficult to expose.

LEADERSHIP SELF-ASSESSMENT

Respond to each statement below with your first thought about how you most often act, not how you think you should or wish you would act. This is intended to help you clarify your strengths as a leader and to aid you in the identification of any areas for your development.

As you read, begin each statement with "I..."

	Seldom				Frequently

Communication

Explain ideas and concepts so all can understand.	1	2	3	4	5
Listen carefully and pay attention to what others say.	1	2	3	4	5
Organize my thoughts and express them clearly.	1	2	3	4	5
Speak with confidence.	1	2	3	4	5

Professional Ethics

Accept responsibility for my actions and decisions.	1	2	3	4	5
Set a proper example for others to follow.	1	2	3	4	5
Demonstrate moral courage by acting on my beliefs.	1	2	3	4	5
Am open, honest, and direct with others.	1	2	3	4	5

Decision Making

Know when to decide myself and when to delegate.	1	2	3	4	5
Build commitment for the decisions I make.	1	2	3	4	5
Include others in decisions that affect them.	1	2	3	4	5
Gather the information necessary.	1	2	3	4	5
Anticipate the impact of a decision on others.	1	2	3	4	5

Planning

Set clear goals and priorities.	1	2	3	4	5
Develop and follow action plans to achieve goals.	1	2	3	4	5
Involve others in planning and implementation.	1	2	3	4	5
Am flexible and adapt my course of action when necessary.	1	2	3	4	5

Solving Problems

Embrace problems and seek to resolve them.	1	2	3	4	5
Know and use tools and techniques for problem analysis and resolution.	1	2	3	4	5
Identify alternative courses of action and analyze them to determine the best approach.	1	2	3	4	5
Focus on solving problems, not fixing blame.	1	2	3	4	5

Entrepreneurship

Seek innovative approaches.	1	2	3	4	5
Actively seek to learn from the "best practices" of others.	1	2	3	4	5
Continually monitor work processes to identify ways to improve them.	1	2	3	4	5
Propose new programs and activities.	1	2	3	4	5

Team Building

Foster collaboration and expect participation in group work.	1	2	3	4	5
Guide the work to enable each member to contribute his or her personal best.	1	2	3	4	5
Am an effective facilitator of group processes.	1	2	3	4	5
Create group synergy that enables the team to achieve effective results.	1	2	3	4	5
Gain consensus from a diverse group.	1	2	3	4	5

(Continued)

LEADERSHIP SELF-ASSESSMENT

As you read, begin each statement with "I . . ."	Seldom				Frequently
Coaching					
Understand and accept my responsibility to coach and help others develop.	1	2	3	4	5
Demonstrate the patience and concern necessary to be an effective coach.	1	2	3	4	5
Clearly state performance expectations.	1	2	3	4	5
Hold others accountable for meeting these performance expectations.	1	2	3	4	5
Leading Change					
Monitor trends and developments to identify changes needed.	1	2	3	4	5
Build commitment to change by informing and involving others.	1	2	3	4	5
Experiment and try new approaches.	1	2	3	4	5
Encourage others to experiment and try new approaches.	1	2	3	4	5
Motivation					
Strive to improve and achieve excellence.	1	2	3	4	5
Am ready to act on opportunities.	1	2	3	4	5
Am optimistic in the pursuit of goals despite obstacles and setbacks.	1	2	3	4	5
Empathy					
Am sensitive to the feelings and needs of others.	1	2	3	4	5
Understand others' feelings and perspectives.	1	2	3	4	5
Am good at sensing emotional currents and the underlying dynamics in relationships.	1	2	3	4	5
Social Skills					
Am adept at influencing and persuading others.	1	2	3	4	5
Have established effective relationships with my colleagues.	1	2	3	4	5
Negotiate and resolve disagreements.	1	2	3	4	5
Work with others toward shared goals.	1	2	3	4	5
Self-Awareness and Regulation					
Manage my own emotions well.	1	2	3	4	5
Gain and keep the trust of others.	1	2	3	4	5
Take responsibility for my performance.	1	2	3	4	5
Am flexible and adaptable.	1	2	3	4	5
Know my strengths and capitalize on them.	1	2	3	4	5
Supervision					
Give clear and concise directions.	1	2	3	4	5
Do not micromanage or over-supervise.	1	2	3	4	5
Do not under-supervise or give too little guidance.	1	2	3	4	5
Interact with those who report to me as much as needed.	1	2	3	4	5
Plan and delegate work appropriately.	1	2	3	4	5

Review your choices to identify:

Areas of Strength:

Possible Areas for Development:

(*Source:* Developed by Maureen Sullivan.)

A number of inventories, including one specifically for librarians,[13] were created to aid leaders in categorizing their own styles and developing strategies for improving their management skills or changing their leadership styles. One technique a leader can use is to temporarily adopt a different style to see how others in the organization react to a variety of styles, the knowledge and recognition of which might help to improve the leader's communication skills.

Ethical Leadership Practice and Social Responsibility

Unethical and/or Illegal Behavior

Leadership, in its broadest sense, encompasses behaviors that are ethical, with attempts to avoid those that might be considered unethical. Furthermore, leaders must recognize and understand the differences between ethics and the law. While ethics relates to a code of morality embraced by a particular person or group, the law is recognized as a system of rules that governs the general conduct of a particular community.[14] Leaders are required to understand both the laws of a situation and the ethical values of the organization and the profession.

People in leadership positions sometimes make false claims to justify certain actions that they have based, conveniently, upon their own point of view to dictate final decisions. They sometimes make decisions without consideration of how the decisions will affect others. Managers who use this approach, remarkably, ignore how they themselves would hope to be treated under similar circumstances. Unethical behavior is just one item in the repertoire that poor and ineffective leaders use to accomplish their goals. Such behavior sometimes includes outright lying, deception, withholding information, and bullying subordinates, both openly and covertly.[15] Ethical behavior is not just reserved for emergencies; it must be constant. Various unethical tactics can be easily recognized, including deliberately creating disharmony among individuals by spreading disinformation, employing unwarranted or unethical criticism, introducing intrusive supervision, enforcing isolation, using humiliation tactics, and singling out a person or persons for different treatment.

Ethical Behavior

The issue of ethical behavior in an information services organization must be addressed as a constant effort of doing the right thing.[16] Simply stated, the process is one of aligning a leader's personal values with subsequent actions within the organization. In an open organizational environment, the focus is on deterring misconduct before it takes place rather than correcting the damage after it has occurred. Honesty and ethics are not just abstract notions but rather guidelines for ethical action. The cliché about "not only doing things right, but also doing

Did You Know?
Aristotle gave us one of the earliest constructs of ethical leadership. According to Peter Northouse in *Leadership: Theory and Practice* (Sage, 2003), Aristotle described the virtues of an ethical person to be courage, temperance, generosity, self-control, honesty, sociability, modesty, fairness, and justice.

the right thing" is at the core of ethics in a professional team. Such ethical leadership is an essential ingredient for a successful library. Effective decision making demands a set of personal ethical responsibilities. It requires leaders to be accountable for the results of what they do, while using their position with due restraint in their actions. When confronted with a questionable situation, it behooves a leader to examine his or her behavior and values before taking an action and to recognize that any subsequent action should reflect those values. Objectivity, respect, openness, trustworthiness, and fairness are the bases of ethical decision making.

To avoid discrimination by making subjective decisions, a good leader always gathers as much knowledge as possible to make objective decisions. A good leader steps back and conscientiously and objectively evaluates the situation or problem before making a decision. He or she will be conscious of the transparency of making the decision, the effect the decision will have on the organization, and whether the decision is fair. A good leader will determine and evaluate the "who, what, when, where, and how" before attempting to resolve an ethical issue. As a follow up to decisions or actions, the leader will publicly disclose the rationality of his or her decisions that affect the work situation.

Ethical leadership involves a moral obligation to not only do the right thing but also do things right. This requires actions and attitudes based in honesty, dignity, fairness, trust, common values, and equity. A simpler, broader definition of the concept of being ethical is to be "fair," especially to those affected by the situation.[17]

Planning for Self-Development

Self-development involves an introspective examination of one's strengths and weaknesses and includes a conscious effort to improve certain areas of one's character and abilities. Leaders who pursue self-development in earnest become more confident and better adept at solving the most complex problems facing an organization. The act of self-development empowers a leader and broadens that person's vision, while experiencing greater job satisfaction and gaining the competencies needed to accomplish missions. Primary developmental activities that foster self-development are the subjects of subsequent chapters.

Among the most frequently recognized competencies for leadership is systems thinking—to see the big picture, to understand the dynamics and interdependencies in a situation, to build relationships based on trust with many diverse individuals, and to manage differences and conflict situations, thereby inspiring and influencing others to achieve cooperative results. Systems thinking requires self-awareness and therefore effective self-management while conveying empathy and compassion toward others, that is, acting as a change catalyst, collaborating with others, and actively fostering such collaborative efforts.

One key ability that runs through this complicated set of competencies is the ability to establish, maintain, and nourish a complex set of relationships with others. This ability can be summarized as being able to lead with vision and purpose and demonstrate a service orientation while developing the self-confidence to deal with political overtones and ambiguity. An effective leader evaluates his or her abilities first, before attempting to lead others. This process of self-evaluation aids in discovering whether one has the competencies necessary to effectively lead. It provides a clearer understanding of one's strengths and weaknesses for assuming or maintaining a leadership role. Only with such understanding can one seriously address ways to overcome identified weaknesses and move on through the continuous process of using self-evaluation to become even more self-aware. *Leadership Practices Inventory*[18] provides a generic tool with which to evaluate and plan one's own leadership development.

"Change" is a keyword for success in information services organizations, because many competing forces are ready to assume what has traditionally been all library and information services organizations' primary mission. These organizations require leaders who can adapt themselves to change by envisioning a successful future and demonstrating a capacity for designing both a strategy and a realistic structure for the future of the organization. This change initiative involves understanding not only the organization but also the external environment that supports or impedes the focus of information services development. It also requires both new and different skills and competencies to remain relevant in today's fast-paced information society. Among the many talents required, some key components for developing visionary leadership can be identified:

1. **Envisioning the future**: The ability to envision a positive future and set attainable goals is paramount to meet the challenges brought about by change. This requires both the knowledge and skills necessary to attain success for an organization as "the" recognized key to the success of its greater enterprise, whatever its primary base: academic, public, school, special private or public organization, or government-supported unit. A visionary leader will have a deep knowledge and understanding of the organization itself and what role it plays in its wider political and social environment. He or she will have imagination, vision, and the ability to set attainable goals. "Visioning" is paramount.

2. **Managing change**: Once the future of the organization has been envisioned, the most important next step is to manage the necessary changes. This requires management skills and a knowledge base—educational, political, and social—to position the organization for a successful future. It involves environmental scanning: developing a community profile, conducting information needs analyses, recognizing a technological impact, identifying current and prospective financial support, etc. Maintaining staff involvement and rewarding innovative initiatives of staff, as well as eliciting community support, both ethical and financial, are vital to any plan for future success.

> **RECOMMENDED RESOURCE**
>
> *The Systems Thinking Playbook* by Linda Booth Sweeney and Dennis Meadows (Sustainability Institute, 2008; available from **www.pegasuscom.com**).

3. **Listening and learning**: One of the key attributes of a leader is regularly seeking feedback from staff and users, as well as financial supporters, regarding the organization's services to promote better performance. This, of course, includes aspects of mentoring the next generation of leaders and requires a commitment to leading, establishing effective avenues of communication, and developing trust within the information services organization and its wider community.

Developing Self-Confidence

Among the various traits, skills, abilities, and characteristics that potential leaders might identify and emulate, perhaps the most important one is that of developing self-confidence. Decisive leaders demonstrate self-confidence by remaining calm, collected, and committed when they introduce new things, when they seek financial and other support from outside the organization, as well as when they teach and mentor others. Additionally, leaders must demonstrate empathy and be accountable for actions taken. With this approach they will earn the trust and respect of others, thereby furthering their sense of self-confidence. Self-examination, on the part of successful leaders, reveals effectiveness as well as gaps in decisions made about important issues within the organization. Additionally, self-efficacy reveals leaders' capabilities in exercising influence over others. This is the fundamental basis from which leadership develops and confidence is established to make decisions that precipitate actions. Generally, people don't listen to managers who are unsure of themselves.

Through the process of self-examination, evaluating personal strengths and weaknesses, leaders develop the ability to understand their own emotions and to recognize the effects their emotions have on work performance and working relationships. Leaders demonstrate self-confidence when they are decisive, when they stay calm in the midst of chaos, when they try new things, when they teach and mentor others, and when they perform the many other functions essential to leadership. Optimism and enthusiasm usually have roots in self-confidence through which those who possess it subconsciously examine their beliefs about their effectiveness in performing specific tasks. Such self-efficacy plays an important role in the general level of self-confidence. Although it is a somewhat intangible quality, it is easily recognized when demonstrated in building self-confidence, which in turn creates a mind-set for trying new things that are opportunities for developing self-efficacy. When examined carefully, three attributes can be identified:

1. **Self-confidence**—in which attitudes, skills, and values are combined to produce positive results, both attitudinal and action oriented

2. **Self-control**—by managing those actions and communicating in an appropriate way so that hoped-for results can be met

3. **Compassion**—by listening to others in the organization and responding in an appropriate and timely manner

All of these depend on good communication skills. They also require a commitment to setting an example. Several skills and attributes are obvious in this development:

- Thinking positively, being optimistic, and developing good mentoring skills
- Creating a motivating environment and working with demonstrated optimism and determination
- Developing decision-making skills that create and enhance a higher level of confidence and satisfaction in the work environment
- Observing and learning from others' leadership habits and approaches, particularly those who are recognized as being successful
- Effectively handling emotional stress
- Demonstrating integrity by doing the right thing to maintain the confidence of followers
- Networking with staff, colleagues, and peers to remain on top of current developments, attitudes, and issues
- Developing mentoring relationships to benefit themselves, as leaders, and drawing on the talents of those they identify to be visionary leaders and have similar backgrounds and philosophies
- Setting examples to show how things should be done, with integrity and respect from others
- Committing to continuing personal and professional growth

Developing this set of attributes requires the highest level of persistence. All are not only important but necessary attributes in a leader's personal and professional growth. Self-confidence and persistence are required to achieve personal and organizational goals.

The "Teachable Point of View"[19] maintains that a great learning experience occurs when leaders teach their own view and develop a process to convey that viewpoint. The process consists of two activities: (1) development of a teachable point of view, i.e., a description of what it takes to be successful in an organization and what it takes to lead others; and (2) the creation of a dynamic and living story to convey the teachable point of view. It involves four areas of leadership: ideas, values, edge, and emotional energy.

Notes

1. Collins, Jim. 2001. *From Good to Great: Why Some Companies Make the Leap and Others Don't*. New York: Harper-Collins.
2. Library Leadership Network. Available: lln.lyrasis.org (accessed February 5, 2010).

EXERCISE

Develop Your Teachable Point of View

Noel Tichy and Patricia Stacey formulated what they call the "Teachable Point of View" approach. They found that the most powerful learning experiences in leadership development occurred when leaders taught their own points of view.

The process consists of two important activities: development of a teachable point of view (a description of what it takes to be successful in the organization and what it takes to lead others) and the creation of a dynamic and engaging story to convey the teachable point of view.

The teachable point of view has four critical leadership areas: ideas, values, edge, and emotional energy. The following outline invites you to begin to develop your own teachable point of view.

Ideas

- What are your ideas about the future for libraries, for your library?
- What will make the library successful?
- What does the library do to create value for its constituents?
- What might it do?

Values

- What are the values of your library—the ones the library lives by?
- How do these values support the library's work to create value for its constituents?
- Are any of these values likely to impede future efforts to create value for its constituents?

Edge (an unflinching readiness to face reality and the courage to act)

- What tough issues are you dealing with? What are the critical decisions you face?
- What holds you back?
- What might be the consequences of delayed decision making?

Emotional Energy

- What do you do to keep yourself energized?
- Think of a time when you generated positive energy in a situation. What effect did this have?
- What do you do to motivate others?

Your Teachable Point of View

Reflect on what you have written so far.

- What does it take to be successful in your leadership practice?
- What is required to motivate and lead others?

Your Leadership Story

Develop your story around these three elements:

1. The case for change—why things cannot continue as they are
2. Where we are going—the picture of a better future
3. How we will get there—what we will have to do, stop doing, do differently to create a better future

3. Bennis, Warren, and Bert Nanus. 1985. *Leaders: Four Strategies for Taking Charge.* New York: Harper & Row.
4. Davenport, T., and Larry Prusak. 1991. *Working Knowledge.* Boston: Harvard Business School Press, p. 5.

5. Stueart, Robert D., and Barbara B. Moran. 2007. *Library and Information Center Management*, 7th ed. Westport, CT: Libraries Unlimited, p. 298.

6. "Key Competencies." British Columbia Leadership Management Institute. Available: www.leadingfutures.ca/files/r-comps.pdf (accessed February 5, 2010).

7. Stueart, Robert D., and Barbara Moran. 2007. *Library and Information Center Management*, 7th ed. Westport, CT: Libraries Unlimited, p. 95.

8. "Leadership and Emotional Intelligence Assessments." MySkillsProfile: Global Online Assessment. Available: www.myskillsprofile.com/tests.php?test=22 (accessed February 5, 2010); Marsick, Victoria J. and Karen E. Watkins. 2003. "Demonstrating the Value of an Organization's Learning Culture: The Dimensions of the Learning Organization Questionnaire." *Advances in Developing Human Resources* 5, no. 2: 132–151.

9. Maccoby, Michael. 1981. *The Leader*. New York: Simon & Schuster, p. 14.

10. Kouzes, Jim, and Barry Posner. 2003. *Leadership Practices Inventory*, 3rd ed. New York: Wiley.

11. Goleman, Daniel, Richard Boyatzis, and Annie McKee. 2002. *Primal Leadership*. Boston: Harvard Business School Press.

12. Naughton-Travers, Joseph. "Understanding Your Leadership Style and Building Your Leadership Skills." Atlanta: Open Minds (November 29, 2007). Available: www.naatp.org/secad/2007_presentations/JNT%20UnderstandingYourLeadershipStyle10-24-07%20pd.ppt#63 (accessed February 5, 2010).

13. Gray, Brian. *Self-Awareness: The Key to Leading Others*. The Library & Information Science Professional's Career Development Center. Available: www.liscareer.com/gray_self.htm (accessed February 5, 2010).

14. McCrimmon, Alice. 2007. "What Does It Mean for Leadership to Be Ethical?" In *Social and Cultural Foundations of American Education*, edited by Dwight W. Allen, Patrick M. O'Shea, and Peter Baker. Available: en.wikibooks.org/wiki/Social_and_Cultural_Foundations_of_American_Education (accessed February 5, 2010).

15. Herd, Jeff. 2008. "Is There a Place for Ethics in the Library?" *ACCESS* 22, no. 4: 5–8.

16. "Code of Ethics of the American Library Association." Chicago: ALA (as amended January 22, 2008). Available: www.ala.org/ala/aboutala/offices/oif/statementspols/codeofethics/codeethics.cfm (accessed February 5, 2010).

17. Heim, Kathleen M. 1991. "Human Resources Management: Ethics in Personnel." In *Ethics and the Librarian*. Urbana-Champaign, IL: University of Illinois, p. 110.

18. Kouzes and Posner, *Leadership Practices Inventory*.

19. Sullivan, Maureen. "Leadership Development: A Teachable Point of View." Available: lln.lyrasis.org (accessed February 5, 2010).

Influencing and Persuading Others

The leader's job, after all, is not to provide energy but to release it from others.

— Frances Hesselbein

Understanding Influence, Power, and Persuasion

The quality of leadership determines the culture of an organization and, ultimately, the success of the organization. The heart of effective leadership is the ability to influence and persuade others. A leader's ability to effectively and consistently influence and persuade people depends on developing open and trusting relationships with them. Leaders foster trust when they are open, honest, and direct in their communication, when their behavior is consistent with their stated expectations, when those expectations are based on a vision for the organization, when they respect diversity, when they develop a realistic sense of their own strengths, when they handle difficult situations with diplomacy and are consistent in their actions, when they are authentic in their interactions with others, and when they set an example for others to emulate. Passion is a term often used to describe a consummate leader. Such genuine engagement over time causes followers to perceive the leader to be reliable and credible. Because every employee potentially has an opportunity to become a leader, each has the opportunity to not only impact but learn from the leadership skills of others.

Richard Boyatzis and Annie McKee take the concept of influencing and persuading to a deeper level and incorporate it into what they call *resonant leadership*. They describe resonant leaders as being "in tune with those around them. This results in people working in sync with each other, in tune with each others' thoughts (what to do) and emotions (why to do it). Leaders who can create resonance are people who either intuitively understand or have worked hard to develop emotional intelligence—namely, the competencies of self-awareness, self-management, social awareness, and relationship management. They act with mental clarity, not simply following a whim or an impulse."[1]

They propose three key components:

1. **Mindfulness**: being fully aware of all that one experiences *inside the self*—body, mind, and spirit—and paying full attention to one's surroundings—the people, the natural world, and the events

2. **Hope**: maintaining clear thoughts about what the future can be and how to get there, incorporating the emotions of optimism, excitement, and compassion and the abilities to dream and have aspirations

3. **Empathy**: combining actions with a caring attitude

Other adjectives are applicable as well: inspiring, reasoning, and even being persuasive. All of these require self-awareness. Leaders who are trustworthy and practice resonant leadership build relationships that enable them to influence others. This influence is critical to effective day-to-day performance and to innovation and performance improvement. Of course, the fine line between "influencing" and "manipulating" must be carefully maintained. Primary factors in the process of becoming a resonant leader are to subject oneself to self-examination and to clarify one's objectives, thinking, and work-related values.

Styles of Influence

Leonard D. Goodstein[2] provides this distinction between power and influence:

> Power refers to the capacity of a person to produce some desired behavior in some other person...; power involves some kind of direct command or requirement for action. Influence, on the other hand, refers to the means that are used to produce desired behavior in the absence of power....Whenever a power relationship exists between individuals or groups, an influence relationship also exists; influence relationships, however, are not dependent on power relationships. Indeed, people can even influence those who have power over them.

Many are familiar with the various strategies used to influence others in the workplace. They include Position authority ("I am the manager"), Prodding through threats ("If you don't do it my way, then..."), Rewarding ("If you do it my way, then..."), and Persuading (with arguments difficult to deny). Many authorities on organizational behavior have examined these tactics.

Kipnis and Schmidt conducted an extensive survey of managers to identify the behaviors that enabled them to influence others. Based on their factor analysis of the tactics used, they identified eight general categories of influence: assertiveness, ingratiation, rationality, sanctions, exchange of benefits, upward appeal, blocking, and coalitions. Kipnis and

Schmidt's Profiles of Organizational Influence Strategies (POIS)[3] are the basis of a self-assessment instrument designed to help respondents clarify their preferred styles of influence.

Hay Group offers its Influence Strategies Exercise (ISE). It is based on more recent research conducted by McBer & Company and consists of nine influence strategies:[4]

1. **Empowerment**: making others feel valued by giving them praise, credit, and recognition and by involving them in decision making and in the planning and implementation of one's ideas

2. **Interpersonal awareness**: identifying other people's concerns and positioning one's ideas to address these concerns

3. **Bargaining**: gaining support by offering to exchange favors or resources, by making concessions, or by negotiating to a mutually satisfactory outcome

4. **Relationship building**: taking time to get to know others personally and to maintain friendly communication with them so that they will be inclined to support one's ideas in the future

5. **Organizational awareness**: building support for one's ideas by identifying and getting the support of the key people who can influence others within the organization

6. **Common vision**: showing how one's ideas support the organization's broader goals or values or appealing to higher principles such as fairness

7. **Impact management**: thinking carefully about the most interesting, memorable, or dramatic way to present ideas in order to gain people's support

8. **Logical persuasion**: using logical reasons, facts, and data to convince others or using knowledge or expertise to persuade

9. **Coercion**: using threats, punishment, or pressure to get others to do what one wants

Hay Group's self-assessment exercise is accompanied by a booklet of interpretative notes that describe each of the nine influence strategies in specific terms. It also includes an assessment of when each style is likely to be effective and when it is not.

A key source of power for managerial leaders is the authority of their position. One can never be an effective manager without wielding some influence on those they supervise. When influence is exercised with care and founded in trust it will lead to commitment and establish what some would call "power." However, when influence is used arbitrarily and with followers one has no relationship of trust with, the result is likely to be compliance, not commitment. Failure to influence can easily lead to managerial ineffectiveness. It is therefore critical that managerial leaders practice resonant leadership and actively build trust in their coworker relationships.

Both managerial leaders and those who lead from any position have personal power. Personal power is the ability of an individual to

---

QUICK TIP

This self-assessment, "Influence Strategies Exercise (ISE)," is available from **www.haygroup.com**.

accomplish or get what he or she wants in a situation, given what is possible and/or available. Individuals vary in the extent to which they have and exercise personal power. To be successful in the exercise of power, individuals must:

- be clear about their objectives,
- assume self-responsibility for acting to achieve these objectives,
- know what is possible and attainable in a given situation,
- be open and clear in communications with others,
- remain focused on the desired results,
- decide how to proceed and take responsibility for their actions, and
- remain aware of how their words and actions affect others.

In today's organizations, where so much of the work to be done requires collaboration and calls for informal leadership, influence is the key to getting results. As more managerial leaders recognize that leadership can happen from any position and that the capacity for leadership exists in every staff member and in most challenging situations, meaningful empowerment throughout the organization is increasingly important. A culture of empowerment is one in which influence is exercised between and among individuals of different ranks, across unit boundaries, and whenever one individual or group causes another to accomplish a result. In the empowered organization influence is ubiquitous. This empowerment recognizes that there are three interacting and mutually supportive spheres of influence: the empowered individual, the empowered manager, and the empowered organization.

Tactics for Persuasion

Jay Conger[5] makes the case for managerial leaders to learn what he calls the "necessary art of persuasion" and suggests that persuasion occurs when a leader answers the question, "Why should I do it?" Conger describes four essential steps to effective persuasion:

1. **Establish credibility**: Credibility is the result of two key factors: expertise and relationships. Expertise derives from demonstrated competence and knowledge and a consistent pattern of sound judgment and effective decisions. Relationships based on trust and on active, open, supportive, and direct communication cause others to be persuaded.

2. **Find common ground**: Take time to understand those whom you want to persuade. Learn their needs, desires, values, beliefs, and goals. Frame what you want to achieve to appeal to these.

3. **Provide evidence**: Once credibility is established and the common ground is framed, the ability to persuade becomes a matter of presenting information and evidence. It is especially important

---

EXERCISE

Draw three concentric circles on a piece of paper. Put yourself in the innermost circle and label it "where I have control"; label the next one out "where I have direct influence"; and label the outermost circle "where I may have influence." Now complete the diagram by filling in each circle with the individuals, groups, and activities that are appropriate to each.

(*Source*: This activity is adapted from Stephen Covey's "Circles of Influence.")

to provide relevant and useful data and information. Conger maintains that the inclusion of vivid examples, metaphorical language, and analogies is essential to make the case come alive for the intended audience. He argues that the power of language in the art of persuasion cannot be underestimated.

4. **Connect emotionally**: This involves conveying a personal commitment to one's own position, reading one's audience accurately to discern their emotional state, and using language and tone in a way that will resonate with the language and tone of the audience. This is resonant leadership in practice.

Personal Power and Influence

Persuasion is the process of moving others by argument to a position or course of action either temporarily or permanently.[6] This process occurs in a series of stages, each with a set of tactics to be employed for success:

1. **Preparation**: Lay the groundwork by setting a tone of positive anticipation.

   - Anticipate and prepare for resistance. Think about what questions or issues will be raised, and prepare appropriate responses.

   - Gather information and examples from other similar situations.

   - Plan a powerful presentation.

   - Ask yourself: is this doable and worth doing?

2. **Presentation**

   - Devise an effective opening, a way to engage the audience right away.

   - Use visuals, images, metaphors, and analogies to paint a vivid picture.

   - Present the potential risks and downsides. Be open and direct about them.

   - Encourage discussion. Engaging discussion is the best means to develop commitment. Assure the audience that the idea is doable and beneficial. Explain why.

3. **Implementation**

   - Reach agreement on how to assess success.

   - Monitor progress.

   - Focus on accomplishments.

   - Face problems head on. Avoid being defensive when setbacks and problems occur. Stay focused on moving forward.

   - Take time to identify the real causes of problems before jumping to solutions.

**Preparing to Persuade:
Some Questions to Consider**

What outcome do I want to achieve?

What tactics and approaches have worked for me in the past?

Who will benefit and in what ways if this idea is implemented?

What are the strengths of this idea or approach?

What are its weaknesses?

What objections are likely to be raised? How might I respond?

How will this advance the organization's mission?

What are the probable gains? For me? For others? For the organization?

Who might sponsor this?

How will this lead to improvement?

What is the best way to communicate this to ensure understanding and acceptance early?

- Recognize and express appreciation for individual efforts and contributions.
- Celebrate accomplishments.
- Encourage continuous improvement.

Taken together, these factors can lead to successful implementation of organizational goals.

Notes

1. Boyatzis, Richard E., and Annie McKee. 2005. *Resonant Leadership: Renewing Yourself and Connecting with Others through Mindfulness, Hope, and Compassion.* Boston: Harvard Business Press, p. 4.
2. Goodstein, Leonard D. 1981. "Getting Your Way: A Training Activity in Understanding Power and Influence." *Group & Organization Studies* 6, no. 3 (September): 283–284.
3. Kipnis, David, and Stuart M. Schmidt. "POIS: Profiles of Organizational Influence Strategies." Menlo Park, CA: Mind Garden. Available: www.mindgarden.com/products/pois.htm (accessed February 8, 2010).
4. "Influence Strategies Exercise." Philadelphia: Hay Group. Available: www.haygroup.com/leadershipandtalentondemand/Products/Item_Details.aspx?ItemID=54&type=7&t=2 (accessed February 26, 2010).
5. Conger, Jay A. 1998. "The Necessary Art of Persuasion." *Harvard Business Review* (May–June): 84–95.
6. Association of College and Research Libraries. 2006. *The Power of Persuasion: Advancing the Academic Library Agenda from the Front Lines.* Chicago: ACRL, p. 9.

Building and Leading Groups and Teams

It is amazing what can be accomplished when nobody cares about who gets the credit.

— Robert Yates

Why Group and Team Work Is Important

The use of teams and groups as work units has increased in the past decade in library and information services organizations. Many of these organizations have redesigned their procedures to enable staff to work in teams. Most have used a variety of groups, including ad hoc task forces and project management teams, to help resolve major work-related issues. Team leaders, who often are managerial leaders in their organizations, play a very important role in the development of these groups and teams, so it is essential that they become skillful in developing high-performing teams.

Katzenbach and Smith offer the best definition of a team: "A team is a small number of people with complementary skills who are committed to a common purpose, set of performance goals, and approach for which they hold themselves mutually accountable."[1] The leader's role in building a team is to facilitate the group's development through a series of sequential stages. One simple and popular description of this process is (1) Forming, (2) Storming, (3) Norming, and (4) Performing:

Stage 1: Forming: Individual orientation behavior is driven by a desire to be accepted by the others and to avoid controversy or conflict. This comes with the initial appointment of the team, getting to know each other, and reviewing the statement of the charges.

Stage 2: Storming: Some conflict and polarization around interpersonal issues occurs. People's patience will break early, and minor confrontations will arise that are quickly dealt with or glossed over. This occurs when the members begin to address

IN THIS CHAPTER:

✔ Why Group and Team Work Is Important

✔ Understanding Group Dynamics

✔ How Groups Become Teams

✔ Facilitating Group and Team Work

✔ Guiding Consensus Decision Making

✔ Cooperation as the Basis for Synthesizing the Wisdom of Groups the issues, including both those of the eventual outcome of their deliberations as well as the interpersonal ones.

Stage 3: Norming: Group feeling and cohesiveness develop. New standards evolve, and the "rules of engagement" for the group become established. The scope of a group's tasks or responsibilities is clear and agreed on. The team members have overcome some of the initial issues, interpersonal and context related, and begin to take responsibility for both their personal actions and the outcome of their efforts.

Stage 4: Performing: Group energy is channeled into the work to be done. Group identity, loyalty, and morale are all high. Everyone is equally task focused and relationship focused. This occurs when the team comes together and becomes adept at making decisions and proposing solutions.[2]

Often a fifth stage, that of Adjourning, is appropriate. In this final stage the group reaches closure. The work comes to an end. Individuals are proud of having achieved much and are glad to have been part of such an enjoyable and rewarding experience.

Team leaders monitor the team's progress, both in work accomplishment and in the development of effective relationships and real collaboration. Among the diagnostic questions that the team leaders can use in their work are these:

1. Has a clear and meaningful purpose for the team's work been established? Is there a set of stated performance goals that can be agreed on?

2. Are the interpersonal and technical skills of the members sufficient to achieve the team's goals?

3. Is the team appropriate in size to allow for interchange of ideas and information?

4. Has the organization provided appropriate avenues of communication, both personal and technological?

5. Is the team leader experienced with or capable of leading the group in successfully achieving stated goals?

6. Are the goals stated in measurable or observable terms so that successful, progressive steps can be taken?

7. Has a realistic timeframe been established in order to carry out the work of the team?

Understanding Group Dynamics

Simply bringing a group of people together to address an organizational need or issue does not automatically bring a successful outcome. Observing the group closely, you might recognize several different behavioral patterns and roles: one person might take the lead in the conversation, offering his or her thoughts and opinions freely. This person

---

EXERCISE

Identify a group or team with which you currently work. At what stage is this group or team now? Why? What steps might be taken to advance the development of this group?

QUICK TIP

The most important and easiest to learn tool for facilitating group and team work is the agenda. An effective agenda lists the topics or activities to be addressed, the purpose of each (information, discussion, or decision), and the time estimate.

FACILITATING DISCUSSION: GENERAL GUIDELINES

Start the session: Welcome the participants, introduce yourself, and briefly review the purpose of the discussion.

- Present a set of ground rules or guidelines for the discussion, and test for agreement with the participants.
- Open the discussion with a general, broad question.
- Encourage everyone to participate.
- Ensure balanced participation. Be alert to who is ready to speak, and call on them.
- Remain neutral on the content of the discussion.
- Practice active listening.
- Encourage the expression of different points of view.
- Help participants understand each other and their different perspectives.
- Periodically summarize the progress.
- Record key points or ideas. A flip chart is an effective tool for this.
- Manage time. Be alert to the progress of the discussion and the time remaining.
- Invite the "reflective observers" to comment.

Bring the session to a close: When about five minutes remain, pause and ask if there is anything else anyone wants to say before you move to closure and adjournment. Summarize the key points. Finally, thank everyone for his or her participation and adjourn.

---

might appear to be the self-appointed leader. Another person might be observed in heated disagreement with the first, interrupting frequently and arguing a point, while a third appears to be deeply concerned about hurting others' feelings by making any opposing statement. Additionally, there is, perhaps, one individual who remains quiet out of concern about hurting feelings and wanting to make everyone feel that each one's point is a good one. These are but a few of the behaviors and roles that people assume in group settings.

Of course, in a formal committee or team, a great deal depends on the task at hand and the knowledge and skills of the members. Team building is a process that must be nurtured. Understanding interpersonal dynamics is just as important as having knowledge of the issue at hand. It is important to build ownership, to communicate effectively, and to gain the commitment of every team member in order to achieve the goals and objectives of the process. Therefore, competency in team building is critical to effective leadership because it improves morale; fosters cohesiveness, collaboration, and commitment; increases individual motivation; and contributes to individual growth and development. This work of a leader requires:

1. clarifying the team goals and building ownership/commitment to those goals across the team, thereby establishing the fundamental principles for the work;
2. identifying any and all issues that inhibit the team from reaching its goals and removing those inhibitors; and

Did You Know?
The key skills for ensuring an effective discussion are opening the discussion, listening, seeking clarification, ensuring balanced participation, summarizing key points, managing time, keeping the discussion on track, identifying and managing differences, and providing an effective summary and closure before adjournment.

3. putting in place "enablers" to help facilitate the goals to be achieved at high standards, including vision, commitment, inclusion, and consensus building.

How Groups Become Teams

A team is a group of people who work together effectively toward a common, clear goal, and team building is an effort that enables them to reach it. Team building activities help organizations improve communication, cope with change, take advantage of individual differences, become supportive and appreciative, and learn how to present creative solutions to vexing problems. Of course, conflicts do often develop, and therefore it is important to establish clear goals that are accepted by every member of the team so that a firm foundation for consensus and commitment is established from the beginning. Some organizations use the Team Diagnostic Survey[3] to discover, expose, and help resolve team differences. It diagnoses how well teams are structured, supported, and led.

Intergroup dynamics must be understood. Interpersonal communication and problem-solving skills are developed in the process. If there appear to be any interpersonal issues among team members, these should be recognized as early as possible and addressed with authority and respect. It is paramount to clarify each member's role and to agree on a set of ground rules so that an atmosphere of honesty and openness can be established from the beginning.

Working together effectively requires consensus on goals, good communication within the team and among members, harmony in member relationships, identification of outside sources that may influence the

---

SOME GENERAL TEAMWORK GUIDELINES

- Work together. Be sure that each member participates and contributes.
- Set aside time to learn about other members' interests, preferences, and talents. This experience is an opportunity for individual development.
- Push for new approaches. Encourage creativity and expression of different approaches and ideas.
- Agree on a set of ground rules for the group to follow. Hold each other accountable for following the ground rules.
- Focus on the big picture—what is in the best interest of the whole organization?
- Focus on the future.
- Use meeting time for discussion and developing ideas.

- Use the time between meetings for additional preparation and background work.
- Encourage and value expressions of difference among various group members. Expect some conflict in ideas and approaches. View this as part of the experience. Conflict often leads to learning, discovery, and better ideas.
- Listen with a view toward understanding.
- Manage yourself so that you are contributing and helping others to contribute.
- Use consensus building to make decisions.
- Set aside some time at the end of each meeting to assess how things are going.
- Ask for help or guidance as needed.
- Have fun and celebrate success.

A SAMPLE SET OF GROUND RULES FOR GROUP DISCUSSION

One of the facilitator's most important tools is to set ground rules or guidelines for the group to follow. This is especially helpful when the discussion time is short. Usually the question "Will everyone commit to following these?" elicits general agreement from the participants.

Consider the group whose discussion you will facilitate, and develop your proposed set of guidelines. Include as many of these as you can:

- Participate and express your ideas.
- Take turns to speak and to listen.
- Listen to understand.
- Expect and respect differences.

- Suspend judgment about the ideas and opinions expressed.
- Be authentic. Say what you mean.
- Think before you speak.
- Be clear and succinct when expressing yourself.

group's work, what each member's responsibilities are in relation to the issue at hand, how to overcome entrenched difficulties, and what the ultimate result of such efforts will be. Through serious and focused discussion, brainstorming, and goal setting, new ideas emerge and team members develop the necessary mutual accountability to accomplish the team's work.

Understanding the dynamics that are characteristic of groups and teams is critical for successful team building. Here are four key conditions necessary for team development:[4]

1. The team must have a **compelling direction**. Someone in authority sets the direction for the team and tells the members what is expected at the end of their work. He or she clearly specifies the outcomes but not the means by which the team is to achieve them. The leader must be challenging and clear without micromanaging the details.

2. The team must have an **enabling structure**. A reasonable-sized team (five to nine members) is necessary to fulfill the objectives of its creation. Often, larger sized teams are created in organizations to fulfill an emotional need rather than a team need. Members must bring the requisite knowledge, skills, and commitment to perform the work.

3. The team needs a **supportive organizational context**. This includes alignment of the education, information, technical, and reward systems to support teamwork. It also includes an information system that provides the team with all the data and background information it needs.

4. At salient moments, the team needs **expert coaching**. The team and its members require timely assistance and guidance. The team leader must provide "challenging, consequential, and clear" leadership. A leader who coaches helps the team to stay focused on its tasks. The team leader ensures that team members understand their roles, responsibilities, and work activities.

The appointment of a competent team leader is essential. A team leader, of course, should have some leadership knowledge and skills. He or she should be adept at goal setting and being able to lead the team toward successful accomplishment of the organization's goals. This means being able to extricate the best performance from each member of the team while creating a sense of team spirit in the process.

Facilitating Group and Team Work

The team leader makes a group or team's work easier by contributing a structure and process within which to work. Effective team leaders have these responsibilities:

- Help a group clarify its main purpose, goals, and objectives.
- Help group members identify their own needs and ways to meet them.
- Guide group discussion to keep it on track.
- Create a positive climate for group discussion.
- Ensure the recording of key points of discussion, decisions, and other notes about the group's work.
- Identify and test assumptions.
- Introduce tools and techniques to advance the group's work.
- Periodically summarize the discussion points.
- Use open-ended questions to stimulate discussion.
- Monitor the group dynamics.
- Ensure full participation.
- Manage differences and conflict with a collaborative approach.
- Provide constructive feedback to enable group members to assess their behavior and make any adjustments.
- Support the group and its individual members.
- Foster shared leadership within the group.

Team members also have a set of responsibilities, and effective leaders will help the members understand and fulfill them. These are effective behaviors for all members of a group or team:

- **Recognize** and respect differences in others.
- **Value** all ideas and contributions made by all members of the team.
- **Listen** and share information pertinent to the team's responsibilities.
- **Ask** questions and attain clarification of pertinent issues.
- **Participate** freely in discussions and make comments when appropriate.

QUICK TIP

Most individuals who are members of groups and teams will respond to an invitation to share their thoughts or perspectives in a discussion. It helps when the team leader periodically invites those who have not yet spoken to do so.

To be effective, team members should understand how to work together—know what behaviors will lead to effective collaboration. To foster such an understanding, some team leaders will begin with a behavioral self-assessment exercise such as the Myers-Briggs Type Indicator[5] or the set of behavioral assessments developed by John Geier (collectively called DiSC). Such exercises help the team to recognize the differences in people's patterns of behavior (which are based on individual interests, reactions, values, motivations, and skills), work styles, and perceptions of situations and how they might ultimately reach conclusions.

The team leader is responsible for laying the groundwork for team activities and for encouraging each team member to articulate his or her own values. These are accomplished within the basic structure of setting an agenda; identifying, when necessary, the roles of specific members; suggesting expected outcomes; initiating and developing ground rules (with group acceptance); facilitating meetings; and monitoring progress while communicating with members along the way.

Given human behavior, it is sometimes difficult for a team to initially come together in a work-related effort. To avoid misunderstandings, when needed some leaders will use the "why/how" technique to resolve basic issues that may be hindering effective communication. This involves a round-robin approach where all members of the team, taking turns, state what is most important to them in this working relationship. The values expressed are discussed in an open, collegial atmosphere. This is not a simple exercise, but rather can serve as a point to be revisited and reinforced should interpersonal issues arise during deliberations.

A group leader is accountable for developing, maintaining, and transforming the group into a team whose decisions are based on consensus, an act that requires unity of action. The round-robin technique will help improve the quality of the members' inputs which in turn will improve the quality of the decision-making process and the decision itself. Addressing any "who, when, what, where, and how" issues as they develop and formulating a plan to resolve them also helps make a group become a team. Brainstorming is another useful exercise in addressing identified problems uncovered in the process of developing solutions.

The transformation tends to empower a sense of self among members, foster cooperation among them, encourage reflective debate, and find common grounds for recommending actions. The transformation process requires an eloquent statement of the mission, potential tasks to address it, and a basis for establishing priorities to create a sense of a shared mission in the process. The team must be able to envision how various actions will fit into the greater organizational efforts. On a basic level, tasks of various members must be identified based on the organization's priorities. Attempts must be made to avoid internal politics by discouraging any we–they discussions and focusing on problems rather than "positions."

Communication between meetings, whether in person or online, is important to the continuing function of addressing the work plan at hand. This also enhances consensus building and coming to closure, producing results, and communicating those results.

RECOMMENDED RESOURCE

For more information on DiSC profile tests, visit **www.DiSCProfile.com**.

QUICK TIP

The round-robin technique is a simple method to ensure that everyone contributes. The team leader or facilitator presents the topic or poses a question and invites each person, in turn, to speak.

RECOMMENDED RESOURCE

The Team Building Toolkit: Tips and Tactics for Effective Workplace Teams, 2nd ed., by Deborah Mackin (New York: AMACOM, 2007) provides excellent tips and tactics for developing effective workplace teams.

QUICK TIP

Brainstorming Basics
- List as many ideas as possible—let the ideas flow.
- Do not critique the ideas as they are expressed. Suspend evaluation until after the list is created.
- Build upon each other's ideas.
- Aim for quantity—the more the better.
- Use a flip chart to record each idea.

TEAM LEADER SELF-ASSESSMENT

This self-assessment provides an opportunity for you to reflect on your experience as a team leader, to identify your areas of current competency, and to consider areas for your development.

1. What types of groups and teams have you led?

2. How experienced do you think you are? Not very, somewhat, quite, or very?

3. What do you enjoy most about facilitating teams and groups?

4. What do you find difficult?

5. Describe a current or recent responsibility:

Group or team: _____

Challenges you face: _____

6. Review the following list of skills and approaches for effective facilitation of group and team work, and rate your current level of competence and confidence in each area using this scale:

> 1 = I have no knowledge or experience in this area.
> 2 = I have some knowledge or experience in this area.
> 3 = I can do this at an average level of competency.
>
> 4 = I am confident in this area.
> 5 = I feel competent and confident in this area to teach someone else.

_____ Understanding the role of the team leader
_____ Understanding the roles people play in groups and teams
_____ Recognizing the characteristics of an effective group or team
_____ Guiding group discussion
_____ Being a process observer
_____ Creating a climate for open discussion
_____ Warming up or getting a group or team started
_____ Handling problem behaviors
_____ Understanding group dynamics
_____ Observing nonverbal signals
_____ Actively listening
_____ Paraphrasing
_____ Checking perceptions
_____ Identifying and testing assumptions
_____ Asking questions

_____ Mediating conflict
_____ Fostering mutual accountability
_____ Building commitment
_____ Creating and using an agenda
_____ Managing time in a group discussion
_____ Developing ground rules or guidelines for group discussion
_____ Encouraging participation in groups
_____ Using the brainstorming technique
_____ Using the round-robin technique
_____ Reaching consensus
_____ Preparing a presentation
_____ Keeping the energy of a group flowing
_____ Getting a group or team to make a commitment
_____ Bringing a group or team's experience to closure
_____ Evaluating how well a group or team worked together

Teamwork fosters success as cooperative methods become developed, with free and open exchange of views that leads to team buy in. The development of a team involves a series of changes through which the individual members become a cohesive and goal-oriented unit. When this occurs, a team becomes an effective unit whose work is accelerated through the team commitment. Observing the teamworking process, one can recognize the changes that occur as the group becomes that cohesive unit. Two sets of skills are required in the process of becoming a cohesive team, these being interpersonal and managerial.

A successful outcome depends on how the team is able to accelerate the process of becoming cohesive. The team's goal requires both equal and constant dedication on the part of each member as well as a clear understanding of the task so that consistency in effort can be maintained. The team leader's or facilitator's primary responsibility is one of keeping every member "on board" and working equally and consistently toward achieving the goals. But it is the group's or team's collective responsibility to mutually decide on directions and outcomes, resolve differences, and maintain momentum and direction. Success depends on this team environment.

It is important to provide open feedback, positive or negative, without prejudice. This, of course, requires frequent discussion of the issues and tasks before the group, not attacks on personalities. If there is criticism, it should be accompanied by a positive suggestion for improvement. Sometimes, when criticism occurs, it is based on opposing views of the group members. As with any other relationship, the differences should be addressed so that common ground can be reestablished and responsibilities refocused.

> The Team Effectiveness Questionnaire (available at **www.firststep management.com/pdf/teq.pdf**) is a tool you can use to explore and discuss aspects of behavior that are found in effective teams.

Guiding Consensus Decision Making

Groups and teams make decisions in a number of ways:

1. **Unanimous agreement**, with everyone reaching the same conclusion. This seldom occurs.

2. **Majority decision**, when half or more agree and/or are willing to accept the decision.

3. **Consensus**, a process whereby all team members reach mutual agreement through active engagement in which all perspectives are expressed and any disagreements are fully discussed.

Consensus requires all members to come to a mutually agreed on course of action that best satisfies the group. It is not a process for determining whose ideas are best, but rather it is a search for the best solution for the group. It operates not by a set of rules or procedures, but rather in a cooperative spirit with the objective of full exploration of an issue until a mutually acceptable solution is found. This occurs through sharing, questioning, testing, and clarifying assumptions and learning from others.

GUIDELINES FOR REACHING A CONSENSUS

- Listen carefully and be open to different ideas.
- Welcome differences of opinion.
- Give everyone an opportunity to offer opinions and points of view.
- Do not vote.
- Identify conflict and disagreement. Talk it through.
- Check for understanding.

Consensus is reached when . . .

Everyone's point of view has been fully heard and considered by the group or team.

The group or team has reached a decision that every member agrees to support.

Everyone can "live" with the decision. All agree that it is the best possible choice.

The "real test" of consensus often occurs later, when others question group members. Ask yourself: when I am questioned about this, will I be able to fully support the decision we have reached?

The process enlists input and ideas from all participants. All ideas are then discussed and synthesized with everyone working together to arrive at a best-possible final group decision. During the process, attempts will be made to overcome the nature of avoidance, denial, and repression of conflict that is often obvious in group efforts. Any diverse elements will be synthesized and incorporated. Consensus does not necessarily mean that everyone thinks the decision made is absolutely the best possible one or even that they believe it might work. What it does mean is that by reaching the decision, no one feels that his or her position was ignored, misunderstood, or didn't receive proper hearing and respect. Everyone has an equal chance to participate, no one dominates the process, and everyone agrees to the final decision.

Consensus building is not just group decision making but rather a group process that requires an open interaction process, commitment to the group approach, effective conflict resolution, and enough time so that all members can participate. In addition, a recognized responsibility to the group is paramount; any member who has trouble with an approach must be prepared to suggest an alternative. Compromise by synthesis is achieved. Both the discussion and the decision can be depersonalized by focusing on the mutual problem. The facilitator, who makes no unilateral decisions and is only one participating member of the group, is responsible for helping the group reach decisions that are the group's will.[6]

Consensus is often confused with "group thinking." Group thinking occurs when everyone agrees with a decision, but some are agreeing only to avoid conflict or because they feel an obligation to. Consensus, on the other hand, occurs when everyone agrees because they think the decision is the best solution to the problem.

Cooperation as the Basis for Synthesizing the Wisdom of Groups

In many ways, team building is like coaching, but for a group rather than for individuals. As stated, the team of colleagues comes together, temporarily, to address an issue facing the organization. As a process it is an ideal way for people who must work well with others to meet the goals of the organization. In the process, they are likely to observe each other's strengths and begin to understand the nature of group dynamics and how to use them effectively.

Team-building exercises are effective ways to foster a positive attitude of working together. Some exercises encourage discussion of how to approach the situation at hand and how the group might ferret out the information needed to address the issue. These exercises facilitate the members' understanding of the importance of group performance. The objective of other types of exercises, such as game playing, is to provide interaction and a common experience that will strengthen the team members' identities. Initial stages in the process of becoming acquainted with each other allow for individuals who work in various organizational units to acquaint themselves with each other and to begin to demonstrate their values and express their opinions.

Open and straightforward communication is the best way for team members to share their thoughts and opinions and therefore allows for decision making to be based on dialogue and not dictatorship. When trust is established within the team, then every member can actively do the work required. This enables cooperation and discourages competition, helps develop a team player and not a loner, and demonstrates the results of cooperative, successful performance.

Notes

1. Katzenbach, Jon R., and Douglas K. Smith. 1993. "The Discipline of Teams." *Harvard Business Review* (March–April): 112.
2. Tuckerman, Bruce. 1965. "Developmental Sequence in Small Groups." *Psychological Bulletin* 63, no. 6: 384–399.
3. Wageman, Ruth, J. Richard Hackman, and Erin V. Lehman. 2004. Team Diagnostic Survey. Available: www.wjh.harvard.edu/~tds (accessed February 3, 2010).
4. Hackman, J. Richard, et al. 2002. "Team Effectiveness in Theory and Practice." In *Industrial and Organizational Psychology: Theory and Practice*, edited by C. Cooper and E.A. Locke. Oxford: Blackwell, p. 118; Hackman, J. Richard. 2002. "New Rules for Team Building." *Optimize* (July): 50.
5. "Myers-Briggs Type Indicator." Available: www.MyersBriggs.org.
6. Schutt, Randy. "Notes on Consensus Decision-Making." Available: www.vernalproject.org/papers/process/ConsensNotes.pdf (accessed February 3, 2010).

Project Management

> Of all the things I've done, the most vital is coordinating the talents of those who work for us and pointing them towards a certain goal.
>
> — Walt Disney

What Project Management Is and Why It Is Important

Many groups and teams work on projects without the benefit of a planned, structured approach to accomplishing their work. Project management provides a formal, disciplined means to design, plan, and implement a project. Martin and Tate's *Project Management Memory Jogger*, one of the best resources for a thorough and practical guide to project management, defines a project to be "any temporary, organized effort that creates a unique product, service, process, or plan."[1]

Managerial leaders in libraries recognize the value of using a project management approach, especially for complex projects such as planning a digital initiative, creating an enterprise-wide strategic plan, or developing a new partnership with a community organization. Project management is a process that calls for clear definition of roles and responsibilities; a well-written and complete project charter; formation of an effective team whose members bring the requisite competencies and commitment; guidance to ensure that the project team learns to work together as a real team; preparation of a project plan that contains all the necessary information to implement the project, including an outline of activities, a list of deliverables, a schedule, a staffing forecast, and a budget; use of planning tools such as Gantt charts and work plans; a means to monitor progress; and a plan for closing the project at completion.

IN THIS CHAPTER:

✔ What Project Management Is and Why It Is Important

✔ Creating Successful Projects

✔ Roles and Responsibilities in Project Management

✔ Forming the Project Team

✔ Writing the Project Charter

✔ Developing the Project Plan

✔ Tools and Techniques for Project Management

RECOMMENDED RESOURCE

The *Project Management Memory Jogger* is available from GOAL/QPC at **www.goalqpc.com**.

The management approach usually occurs in four general stages:

1. Defining the project and its expected outcomes
2. Planning the project, including key activities such as establishing project specifications, identifying resources, setting a timetable, and creating a work plan
3. Executing or implementing the project
4. Evaluating and closing the project

Project management was first developed in the 1960s as a disciplined approach for the U.S. space program. It soon became widely used in government, in the military, and in business. Project management differs from other organizational work in that it focuses on a short-term, temporary effort. Similar to Martin and Tate's definition, given earlier, The Project Management Institute defines a project as "a temporary endeavor undertaken to create a unique project or service."[2] This definition provides an effective means to distinguish project management work from ongoing work processes and performance.

Did You Know?
No two projects are alike. Each project has its own unique requirements, objectives, resources, time frames, and results. Every project has its own set of surprises as well as its own path to conclusion.

Creating Successful Projects

A strong commitment to effective project management methodology and careful planning from the start are critical factors to success. Sponsors and senior administrators have a special responsibility to do all that they can to prepare and enable the project team to carry out its work. Delegation to a project team is one of the most effective ways to engage staff, to enable them to develop new competencies, and to foster a culture of commitment and empowerment in today's workplace. Managerial leaders who assign project teams need to clarify for themselves what will constitute a successful project in their situation. A set of general criteria includes the following:

- A clear and complete charge
- Defined roles and responsibilities and a commitment to accountability
- Effective, competent, and committed team members
- Effective and trusted leadership, skilled in the facilitation of team work
- Specific outcomes that are targeted to customer requirements
- Allocation and effective use of the necessary resources (i.e., project stays within the budget and staffing allocations)
- Adherence to a timetable
- Identification of what has been learned and application of the learning throughout the project

Roles and Responsibilities in Project Management

Martin and Tate offer a model for clarifying the various roles and responsibilities in any project planning effort:[3]

1. Senior Management ensures that the team has a project management process to follow and provides resources.

2. Department Managers support the project objectives and ensure that the team members have the time and other resources necessary to complete the project.

3. The Sponsor ensures that the project has clear direction and support by providing the charter and by ensuring that the project plan meets both customer and organizational needs.

4. The Project Team Leader ensures that the project satisfies both the customers of the project and the organization. The team leader also ensures that the project is completed on time and within its predetermined limits and constraints.

5. Project Team Members make a strong commitment to contribute their personal best to the work. They come to meetings prepared, carry out any assignments between meetings, and hold each other accountable for the work. They ensure that their work satisfies the needs of the project and is completed on time and within budget.

Forming the Project Team

Selecting and preparing a successful project team calls for an understanding of group dynamics and using many of the steps and activities that are essential to the success of any team (see Chapter 4). The following streamlined approach is especially effective for forming a project team:

Step 1: Define the project. Why is it needed? What are the expected outcomes?

Step 2: Carefully consider the need for a team. Some projects are best planned and implemented by an individual or by a couple of individuals. Projects that are complex and address new areas of work are best addressed by a team of individuals who have diverse and complementary competencies. The synergy and innovative thinking that occur in such a group often bring forth high-quality ideas and enable the members to become a high-performing team, especially when guided by a skilled team leader.

Step 3: Select a leader who is able to:
- guide and inspire others;
- manage meetings well;

- facilitate discussion, especially when disagreements occur;
- coordinate work activities;
- communicate well with others;
- bring sound knowledge of project management, both the process and the tools; and
- develop a strong commitment to the successful completion of the project.

Step 4: Select project team members who:

- work well in groups and teams;
- communicate effectively;
- will disagree and can do so constructively;
- will commit to performing the work and doing their best;
- accomplish work on time;
- have a strong interest in and commitment to the goals of the project;
- bring diverse experiences and ideas; and,
- together, will bring a set of complementary skills and abilities.

Writing the Project Charter

The project charter can be developed by the project sponsor, by the project team, or by the sponsor and team together. If the project team develops the charter, the sponsor must approve it before project planning begins. Also, before planning begins, it is important to ask "Who else needs to know or approve this before the work begins?" and ensure that appropriate approval is obtained. These are four key components of a charter:

1. **Project scope statement**: List the project goals and objectives; deliverables, including criteria for these deliverables; boundaries—anything that is outside of the scope of the project; reviews and approvals required; and any other information that will help the project team members understand what they are expected to accomplish.

2. **Project parameters**: Three basic parameters are quality, cost, and time. A successful project achieves quality results and meets customer expectations; is within budget; and is completed on time. The charter therefore should, to the extent possible, spell out the specific requirements or critical dimensions of the project. The *specifications* of quality should be stated. The *budget* to fulfill the cost requirements should be provided. The *schedule* to meet the time requirements should be specified.

3. **Project status reports**: List the reports required and the expected dates of submission.

4. **Project team membership**: List the names and any other relevant information about those who have been assigned to the team (project leader and project team members).

Developing the Project Plan

A good project plan contains many of the elements of any **effective** plan. This stage in the project management cycle requires the **most effort** of the project management team and its leader. This work often has to be accomplished in a relatively short amount of time. One simple, effective approach to a project plan is based on the three requirements or critical dimensions of quality, time, and cost, as described earlier. Planning steps include the following:

- Clarify and confirm the project goals and objectives.
- Determine the results to be accomplished.
- Break the project down into specific activities or steps (work breakdown structure).
- Determine the performance standard for each activity or step.
- Estimate how much time will be required to complete each activity.
- Determine the proper sequence for completion of each activity.
- Identify dependencies (predecessors and successors).
- Identify milestone dates.
- Aggregate this sequence into a schedule for the whole project.
- Determine costs.
- Aggregate the costs into a project budget.
- Determine the staffing needed for each activity, including the level, time, and effort required.
- Identify any policies and procedures that need to be developed.

The key activities to ensure that the requirements for the **quality dimension** are met include the following:

- Specify the performance standards to be met for each activity or component of the project.
- Identify the means for verifying the quality of the performance, e.g., testing, inspection, customer feedback.

To meet the requirements of the **time dimension**, the project team needs to determine three things for each activity:

1. The time it will take to complete each step
2. The earliest point at which a step may be started
3. The latest time by which the step must be started

The usual components of the **cost dimension** are labor, overhead, materials, supplies, and equipment. This work often involves some estimation of amounts in each of the categories but also can be informed by gathering current information about actual costs from reliable sources.

Tools and Techniques for Project Management

As the discipline of project management has evolved in the past 40 years, a number of tools and techniques have been developed to make the work more efficient and productive. Both the Project Management Institute (www.pmi.org) and GOAL/QPC (www.goalqpc.com) are excellent sources for information and guidance for a broad range of tools. We will describe here a select set of the most useful ones for day-to-day library organization.

The **work breakdown structure** (WBS) is an important planning tool in project management. A project management team constructs the work breakdown structure by identifying all of the tasks to be performed—breaking the work down into its component parts—and laying them out in a diagram to represent how they are performed. This diagram then can be used to identify the quality, time, and cost dimensions of each task and work activity.

The **Gantt chart** (named for its developer, industrial engineer Henry Gantt) is a visual display of the major activities in a project and the time duration of each. Each activity is shown as a line on the chart placed to show the time frame in which it will be completed.

The **Program Evaluation and Review Technique** (**PERT**) diagram was created by the U.S. Navy in the 1950s to enable more accurate scheduling of the development of the Polaris submarine. It shows the activities to be accomplished in a time sequence that reveals the dependencies among the activities and any steps necessary to their accomplishment.

A number of software programs are available to support project management. Think carefully before investing not just the money but also the time required to use them.

TOOLS FOR PROJECT PLANNING

Project Planning Form

Complete the following to begin developing a project plan:

1. Write a brief description of the project.

2. Specify the goals of the project. Describe what you want to accomplish.

3. Who are the customers?

4. What are the deliverables for the customers? What will be produced?

(Continued)

TOOLS FOR PROJECT PLANNING *(Continued)*

Project Planning Form *(Continued)*

5. List the specifications for each deliverable. What criteria are customers likely to use to determine their satisfaction with a deliverable?

6. List the activities or steps to follow to achieve the goals and produce the deliverables.

7. What is the desired time frame? When do you hope to complete the project?

Project Charter Template

The Project Charter may be developed by the project sponsor or by the project team, or by the sponsor and team together. If the project team develops the charter, approval by the sponsor is a critical step before the project planning begins. Before the planning begins, it is important to ask, "Who else needs to know or approve this before the work begins?" and then ensure that appropriate action is taken.

Key components of a charter include:

- **Project Scope Statement:** List the project goals and objectives; deliverables, including criteria for these deliverables; boundaries—anything that is outside of the scope of the project; reviews and approvals required; and any other information that will help the project team members understand what they are expected to accomplish.
- **Project Parameters:** The three basic parameters are quality, cost, and time. A successful project is one that achieves quality results and meets customer expectations; is within budget; and is completed on time. The charter, therefore, should spell out the specific requirements, to the extent possible.
  - The *specifications* of **quality** should be stated.
  - The *budget* to be managed to accomplish **cost** requirements should be provided.
  - The *schedule* to be followed to meet **time** requirements should be specified.
- **Project Status Reports:** List the reports required and the expected dates of submission.
- **Project Team Membership:** List the team assignments (project leader and project team members).

Project Planning Work Plan Template

Time Period: From _____ To _____

Activity	Time Duration	Resource Allocation	Responsibility

Notes

1. Martin, Pamela, and Karen Tate. *Project Management Memory Jogger*. GOAL/QPC, Plexus International (1997). Available: www.goalqpc.com/shop_products_detail.cfm?PID=33&PageNum_GetProducts=1&Product ShopBy=7 (accessed February 8, 2010).
2. *A Guide to the Project Management Body of Knowledge*. The Project Management Institute (2000). Available: www.pmi.org (accessed February 26, 2010).
3. Martin and Tate, *Project Management Memory Jogger*, p. viii.

Coaching: Keys to Successful Leadership

> You get the best effort from others—not by lighting a fire beneath them, but by building a fire within.
>
> — Bob Nelson

IN THIS CHAPTER:

✔ Coaching Defined

✔ Skills for Effective Coaching

✔ When Coaching Becomes Counseling

✔ Giving Constructive Feedback

✔ Coaching and Performance Evaluation

✔ Performance Management

✔ Key Steps in the Coaching Process

Coaching Defined

Coaching is an ongoing conversation in which one person, the coach, helps another to improve his or her performance or to solve a problem. The conversation may be formal or informal, and, as discussed later, the process can occur in a supervisor- or manager-to-staff relationship; a colleague-to-colleague relationship; and a staff-to-supervisor or -manager relationship. It is the most important role for the development of others, especially for the development of leadership competence in staff members who work in information services organizations today.

Coaching involves developing strategies to empower individuals to meet organizational goals by helping them to improve performance while at the same time enabling career development. The concept is becoming more important as developing the next generation of leaders in the profession becomes a more complex, yet necessary, activity. The leader's role as a coach is critical to the improvement of individual and organizational performance. The coaching experience in the workplace can best be described as a problem-solving discussion that is directed toward improving or developing different aspects of an individual's performance. It encourages others to analyze their strengths and weaknesses and to challenge their ways of thinking and doing in order to achieve higher levels of performance. In its simplest form, it can occur in a single conversation. However, it usually is understood to be an ongoing process of continuous improvement.

Dennis Kinlaw[1] outlines an effective approach to coaching that extends the coaching process beyond the usual manager–staff relationship to include colleague-to-colleague and staff–boss relationships. Adopting this approach to information services organizations, coaching becomes a key component in the set of important collaborative relationships that are critical to high performance in today's libraries and other information services organizations. Kinlaw defines four different coaching functions. The first three, counseling, mentoring, and tutoring, are directed at solving problems, and the fourth one, confronting or challenging, focuses on improving performance. This format provides a good outline for discussing coaching for information services organizations.

Skills for Effective Coaching

Coaching requires a set of skills, many of which are important to effective communication in any relationship, to ensure that those being coached understand what is expected and are able to follow through to meet these expectations. Among the most important skills are active listening, demonstrating respect and acceptance of others, encouraging and demonstrating open and direct communication, clarifying the problem or situation, helping to identify options, outlining possible consequences of actions, asking effective questions, checking perceptions and assumptions, and giving and receiving feedback. Use the accompanying checklist to review your skills.

When Coaching Becomes Counseling

Counseling is the process managerial leaders use when their efforts to coach staff members have not been successful. Counseling discussions focus on confronting and correcting performance problems and addressing overall substandard performance. It is essential that managerial leaders

---

EXERCISE

Coaching Skills Self-Assessment

Review this checklist to identify the skills you have mastered. Review where you have placed a check mark to confirm that these are competencies you have. Then look at the items you have not checked; these are areas for potential development and ways to strengthen your competence as a coach.

___ Actively listening	___ Clarifying the situation
___ Demonstrating respect and acceptance of others	___ Helping to identify options
___ Offering help and assistance when needed	___ Planning solutions and ways to implement changes
___ Demonstrating care and concern for others	___ Outlining possible consequences of actions
___ Conveying empathy	___ Observing behavior, attending to nonverbal cues
___ Valuing others	___ Asking effective questions
___ Allowing time for venting of feelings	___ Paraphrasing
___ Encouraging and demonstrating open and direct communication	___ Checking perceptions and assumptions
	___ Giving and receiving feedback

Coaching: Keys to Successful Leadership

COACHING AND COUNSELING PROCESSES

Key Steps in Coaching Model

One model for a coaching session for managerial leaders to use with staff is the series of five steps outlined here. These steps provide an effective structure for the conversation, especially when the discussion will focus on a serious problem or when the person to be coached may be resistant to the performance feedback or to the coaching itself.

Step 1: Open the session and spark interest.

- State the purpose of the coaching session.
- Use your planning notes to describe current behavior and offer specific examples.
- Discuss the results and consequences of the behavior.
- Check the staff member's receptivity to what you have described.

Step 2: Ask for the person's response and perspectives.

- Invite the staff member to offer her or his own analysis.
- Probe for reasons for the current behavior.
- Encourage self-assessment and self-discovery.

Step 3: Give your feedback and points of view.

- Acknowledge areas of agreement.
- Point out any areas of concern or disagreement.
- Suggest alternative approaches, if appropriate.
- Reinforce the staff member's responsibility and accountability.

Step 4: Resolve differences. Engage in problem solving.

- Discuss the benefits and possible drawbacks of the different approaches.
- Agree on goals for future performance.
- Begin to plan specific actions.

Step 5: Create a plan of action.

- Get commitment to take action.
- Reach agreement on what will be done and by when.
- Decide when and how to review progress.

Key Steps in the Counseling Process

Step 1: Preparation

- Clarify and carefully define the performance problem or issue.
- Review the steps and schedule in the coaching you have done.
- Review the information you have. Gather any other relevant information.
- Set a time and place for the counseling session. Set aside sufficient time.
- Decide whether or not to have another person join you.
- Tell the staff member why and when you want to hold the discussion.

Step 2: Counseling Conversation

- Begin with a brief review of the purpose and expected outcomes of the meeting.
- Invite questions for clarification.
- Review your concerns, and explain why they need to be addressed.
- Remind the person of previous steps and opportunities given to correct the problem.
- Stress the importance of correcting the situation.
- Invite her or him to identify ways to resolve the problem.
- Reinforce his or her responsibility to do so as soon as possible.
- Remain attentive to her or his attitude and emotions.
- Be calm and remain in control of the session.
- Guide the discussion to reach mutual understanding of the problem and how it will be resolved.
- If appropriate, convey your confidence in the person and provide support.
- Close with a plan for a follow-up meeting.

Step 3: Follow-Up

- Monitor progress.
- Stay in touch with the person and continue regular interaction.
- Meet to check progress.
- Offer honest and specific feedback.

GUIDELINES FOR ACTIVE LISTENING

- Focus your attention on the speaker.
- Be careful to put aside your own thoughts.
- Listen for key messages.
- Avoid judging what the person has to say.
- Consider the ideas and information conveyed.
- Listen with an open mind.
- Watch for your opportunity to comment or to chime in.
- Convey respect and acceptance.
- Manage your own emotions.

Remember that most of us think much faster than we speak. It is natural for us to have our own thoughts come to mind as we are listening to others. Guard against letting these thoughts interfere with the listening process.

---

engage in counseling staff whenever their performance does not meet expectations. Many managers avoid counseling because it takes time and they often want to avoid difficult conversations. Successful managerial leaders recognize the importance of addressing each performance problem as soon as it occurs, especially when performance does not meet clear and established expectations.

Giving Constructive Feedback

One of the greatest challenges leaders face is giving effective and constructive feedback. Many managerial leaders in information services organizations do not do this when needed or on a regular basis. They find it very difficult to communicate information about performance problems and often lack the confidence and the skills to discuss these problems. It is essential that a leader overcome hesitation and develop the self-confidence to initiate and manage difficult conversations with staff—ones in which the skill of giving constructive feedback is used to ensure that staff have the opportunity to correct any problems in their performance. Performance feedback, on both what is working and what is not, is essential to enable staff to perform their work as well as possible.

Effective coaching requires the ability to give constructive feedback in a way that the recipient can both hear the information and at the same time be prompted to act on desirable feedback. Delivery of this feedback requires that a coach:

- Build a relationship with the individual first.
- Position the feedback as a benefit to the person.
- Describe observations about behaviors and conditions, not judgments, about the person.

GUIDELINES FOR FEEDBACK	
Practices for *giving* feedback: • Consider the needs of others. Be sure that your intention is to be helpful. • If the person has not solicited feedback, check to see whether he or she is open to it. • Describe behavior. Avoid interpreting the behavior. • Focus on behavior that can be changed. • Be specific. Avoid generalities. • Give feedback immediately after the behavior or as soon as possible. • Describe how the behavior has an impact on you and on the work situation. • Express your feelings directly. Use an "I statement" to accept responsibility for your own emotions and perceptions. • Check for understanding.	**Practices for *receiving* feedback:** • When you ask for feedback, be specific about the behavior or practice for which you are soliciting the feedback. • Listen to understand. • Try not to respond defensively. Take time to consider the feedback before you respond. The feedback could point to a "blind spot." • Summarize your understanding of the feedback you receive. • If appropriate, share your thoughts and feelings about the feedback and do so in a way that preserves the relationship.

- Be positive—describe what is wanted or expected, not what is not expected.
- Be low key—use a gentle tone of voice.
- Meet in private.
- Offer examples and suggestions for improvement.
- Invite and listen to the individual's perspective.
- Focus on the future—the desired change.
- Reach a mutual understanding of what will change and when.

Coaching and Performance Evaluations

W. Edwards Deming,[2] one of the leading experts on quality improvement of performance in organizations, included annual performance evaluations as one of the Seven Deadly Diseases. He believed that the effects of performance evaluations that focused on the judgment and rating of past performance were "deadly" because they caused fear in those involved and because they did not lead to sustained improvement of performance. Instead, he found that they lead to short-term improvement at the expense of long-term improvement.

In libraries, traditional performance evaluation systems have proven to be somewhat ineffective. Both staff and even supervisors express frustration when using them. There is a constant struggle to find more effective ways of assessing performance. A significant new challenge is that work performance in many situations includes significant new work

---

TIPS FOR EFFECTIVE COACHING

- Actively listen.
- Demonstrate respect and acceptance of others.
- Offer help and assistance when needed.
- Demonstrate care and concern for others.
- Convey empathy.
- Value others.
- Allow time for venting of feelings.
- Encourage and demonstrate open and direct communication.
- Clarify the situation.
- Help to identify options.
- Plan solutions and ways to implement changes.
- Outline possible consequences of actions.
- Observe behavior, attending to nonverbal cues.
- Ask effective questions.
- Paraphrase, when appropriate.
- Check perceptions and assumptions.
- Give and receive feedback.

---

activities. Many staff are called on to perform new work and to learn how to do this work as they are performing it.

Goldsmith[3] proposed that we shift from performance feedback to an approach that focuses on future improvement. Instead of providing feedback on past performance, leaders would provide information and suggestions for future performance and offer guidance and help. Leaders would practice effective coaching on a regular basis. Goldsmith offers the following ten reasons to try his "feedforward" technique:

1. Organizations can change the future, but not the past.

2. It is usually more productive to focus on doing things well and solving problems than to point out what is wrong.

3. Feedforward is especially suited to successful people.

4. Feedforward can be practiced by anyone who is familiar with the work activity. It does not require personal experience with the person.

5. Individuals do not take feedforward information personally (the way they do feedback).

6. Feedforward reinforces the possibility of change. It is based on the assumption that people can make positive changes in their performance.

7. Few of us are effective at giving constructive feedback, and most of us don't like to receive it.

8. Feedforward can address most of what would be covered in the feedback process.

9. Feedforward tends to be more immediate and more effective than feedback. The focus is on offering suggestions and allowing the recipient to decide how to improve.

10. Feedforward can be a helpful tool to apply with any colleague—staff, team members, peers, and managers.

Although feedforward sometimes appears to be an awkward concept, it does suggest an important shift in focus in both philosophy and practice of performance improvement. Most individuals who work in information services organizations today want to be successful contributors. Many face the challenge of learning to do new work and to perform their work in different and more complex ways. Leaders recognize the need for competency development and are increasingly aware of the need to provide training and education to staff at all levels. Learning is truly an integral part of work performance today. Accountability and effective self-management on the part of every staff member is critical to the organization's performance. One can consider several possible approaches by thinking about one of several models, including Goldsmith's feedforward concept.

COACHING PLAN

Person: _____ Date: _____

To ensure that you are well prepared for a coaching session, take time to address these four areas and make notes to yourself:

1. Describe the current behaviors that you want to reinforce or redirect to improve a situation.

2. Identify the specific situation(s) where you observed these behaviors.

3. Describe impacts and consequences of the current behaviors.

4. Identify alternative behaviors and actions to be taken.

Performance Management

Many organizations are replacing traditional performance evaluations with a Performance Management System (PMS). A Performance Management System is an integrated set of processes that supports the utilization and development of an organization's human resources. It is the foundation for two complementary purposes: (1) achieving the organization's overall mission by accomplishing results and (2) establishing an organizational culture that both respects staff contributions to the organization's performance results and values staff development.[4] A Performance Management System will have these nine key components:

1. A competency model that defines the competencies for all work activities
2. A leadership development program to ensure that managerial leaders are able to carry out their role and responsibilities
3. Goal-setting program—a system for specifying both organizational and individual goals (performance plans)
4. Explicit behavioral norms
5. A performance improvement process designed to address any gaps between organizational expectations and individual performance
6. Performance assessment, including 360° feedback processes
7. Coaching
8. A recognition system designed to highlight and express appreciation for individual and team accomplishment
9. Team audits—assessments of team or group effectiveness

COACHING FOCUSED ON TALENT DEVELOPMENT

> Learning is not attained by chance, it must be sought for with ardor and attended to with diligence.
>
> —Abigail Adams (1780)

Research shows that the most effective way to develop leadership competence is through trial and error on the job, an action-learning approach in which coaching can play a crucial role. As discussed in Chapter 1, Warren Bennis recommends exposure to "crucible experiences"—complex, difficult, and challenging assignments that allow individuals to experience deep learning and develop skills and abilities for effective leadership. And, as seen in Chapter 2, Noel Tichy and Patricia Stacey encourage the "Teachable Point of View" approach to leadership development—the most powerful learning experiences in leadership development occur when leaders teach their own points of view. To develop a teachable point of view to assist in coaching endeavors, complete the exercise on page 29.

Key Steps in the Coaching Process

Princeton University Libraries has developed a wonderful toolkit for learning the coaching process. We encourage you to use it as a model to develop your own coaching plan and style.

THE ACADEMIC LIBRARY MANAGEMENT TOOLKIT

Coaching in a Library Setting

Coaching is not merely a technique to be wheeled out and rigidly applied in certain prescribed circumstances. It is a way of managing, a way of treating people, a way of thinking, a way of being.

—John Whitmore, *Coaching for Performance* (p. 18)

What Is Coaching in the Workplace?

The practice of coaching in the workplace is related to sports coaching. Just as an athletic coach helps an individual or a team improve their skills, a workplace coach helps an employee do the best job he/she is capable of. Like athletic coaching, it includes aspects of teaching and training, as well as observation and feedback, but a good workplace coach does not use the command and control techniques that often characterize athletic coaching.

Coaching is different from therapy or counseling because it doesn't explore a person's private life and it is not a healing art. It is strictly workplace and behavioral based. It looks to the present and future, rather than dwelling on the past.

Additional Workplace Communication Formats

(with a lot of coaching overlap, of course)

- Informational meetings
- Casual conversations and feedback
- Giving advice
- Disciplinary conversations
- Formal performance appraisals

When and Why to Coach

When is coaching appropriate?

- To introduce new employees to the institutional culture
- For career development
- To introduce new tasks or procedures
- For process improvement
- To implement organizational changes
- For motivational purposes
- To correct an employee's unsatisfactory performance

The Benefits of Good Coaching

- Helps develop employee competence
- Fosters productive working relationships
- Provides opportunities for conveying appreciation
- Fosters self-coaching behaviors
- Improves employee performance and morale
- Helps diagnose performance problems
- Helps correct unsatisfactory or unacceptable performance
- Helps diagnose a behavioral problem
- Helps correct unsatisfactory or unacceptable behavior
- Produces a more positive workplace environment

(Continued)

THE ACADEMIC LIBRARY MANAGEMENT TOOLKIT *(Continued)*

How People Learn: The Importance of Experience

Numerous studies, including ones at IBM and the U.K. Post Office, have shown that people recall more of what they learn the more actively involved they are in the learning process.

	Told	Told and shown	Told, shown, and experienced
Recall after 3 weeks	70%	72%	85%
Recall after 3 months	10%	32%	65%

Coaching, as a teaching mode, falls more toward the *Told, shown, and experienced* end of this spectrum. Experience leads to awareness and engagement, which in turn lead to responsibility and change.

Two-by-Two Coaching Sample

Scenario

Some librarians complain—among themselves and to the new manager—about a librarian coworker. They say Wilfred has not carried his weight in the department for years. No one has spoken directly with Wilfred about this, however. The new manager, Glenda, finds that the work group does not know how to effectively manage other routine conflicts as well. Glenda knows that coaching may take a while, but the complaints have presented an opportunity for it. She will begin coaching individuals and modeling how to effectively resolve typical interpersonal conflict.

Factors to Consider

- More than a dozen people involved
- Varying levels of interpersonal competence
- Need to ameliorate the day-to-day situation quickly
- Need for long-term improvement in work climate

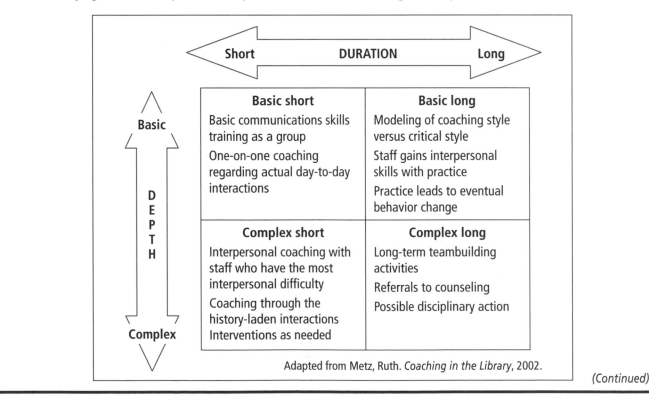

Adapted from Metz, Ruth. *Coaching in the Library*, 2002.

(Continued)

THE ACADEMIC LIBRARY MANAGEMENT TOOLKIT *(Continued)*

Preparing for a Formal Coaching Session

Prepare Yourself

Be sure that you are calm and have clarified the following points in your own mind:

- What is the message about?
- What is the background of the message?
- Why is it important to you?
- Why is it important to the recipient?
- Why is it important to the Library?
- How will the message be of benefit to the person who receives it?
- How urgent is the situation?

Prepare the Setting

- Is it comfortable?
- Does the seating arrangement promote a collaborative atmosphere?
- Have you arranged for time with no interruptions?
- Do you have all the documentation you need?
- Do you have materials to take notes?
- Is the person to be coached in the right frame of mind?

Questioning

Purpose of Questions

- Solicit information, input, ideas.
- Engage the mind and senses of the employee.
- Help employee reflect and become aware.
- Help employee assume responsibility.
- Demonstrate respect and inclusiveness.

Questioning Technique

Good questions are brief, clear, focused, relevant, constructive, neutral, and open-ended.

To get better responses to your questions:

- Tell employees what's at stake, why you need this information.
- Give employees time to think about their responses.
- When you're done asking, be quiet and listen.

Questioning for Corrective Coaching Sessions

State why the behavior needs changing.

Who should be responsible for suggesting solutions? You may choose to put the burden:

- on the employee ("What can you do to keep this from happening again?"),
- on both of you ("Is there something I can do to help?"), or
- on the process ("How can we work this out?").

Listening

Listening Technique

- **Receive**
  To understand it, you have to hear it. Prepare. Be still. Wait. Don't assume. Take notes. Probe gently and redirect the conversation if necessary. Concentrate on the speaker to maintain your focus. Practice the art of doing one thing well.

(Continued)

THE ACADEMIC LIBRARY MANAGEMENT TOOLKIT *(Continued)*

Listening Technique *(Continued)*

- **Reflect**
  Think about what you're hearing. Make sense out of it. Put it into a meaningful context. Ask questions as you need to. Listening is an active process.

- **Rephrase**
  Bounce what you're hearing back to the source; rephrase to make sure you're getting it right. Use the echo back technique.

(Source: Developed by Luisa R. Paster, Training and Development Specialist, Princeton University. Used with permission.)

Notes

1. Kinlaw, Dennis C. 1999. *Coaching for Commitment, Problem-Solving Skills Questionnaire: Interpersonal Strategies for Obtaining Superior Performance from Individuals and Teams*, 2nd ed. New York: Jossey-Bass.
2. Deming, W. Edwards. 2009. *Out of Crisis*. Cambridge, MA: MIT Press.
3. Goldsmith, Marshall. 2002. "Try Feedforward Instead of Feedback." *Leader to Leader* (Summer). Available: www.linkageinc.com/thinking/linkageleader/Documents/Marshall_Goldsmith_Try_Feedforward_Instead_of_Feedback_1102.pdf (accessed February 9, 2010).
4. Rollo, James. 2001. *Performance Management: A Pocket Guide for Employee Development*. Salem, NH: GOAL/QPC, Competitive Advantage Consultants, Inc.. Available: www.goalqpc.com (accessed March 16, 2010).
5. Tichy, Noel, and Patricia Stacey. 1997. *The Leadership Engine*. New York: Harper-Collins.

Mentoring

The more you loose yourself in something bigger than yourself, the more energy you will have.

— Norman Vincent Peale

Mentoring Defined

Mentoring, in its more traditional sense, is an interaction between a more experienced person and another less experienced individual. In an organizational setting, it includes an effort to provide guidance to motivate the mentored person (the term used in this discourse is "protégé" although "mentee" is sometimes used) to take positive actions to benefit the organization. In this regard, it is a human resources enhancement process within an organization not simply for career development but also for workplace learning and benefit. Mentoring is one of the most powerful methods by which an organization's future can be shaped. A mentor performs a variety of roles, including those of sponsor, counselor, coach, role model, developer of competencies and talent, promoter of professional activities and engagement, confidant, challenger, positive role model, opener of doors, developer of careers, and teacher.

In its historical context, mentoring is a specialized form of developing individuals in both informal, personal relationships and in more formal career-developing, work-related relationships. A mentor can be viewed as a wise and trusted advisor and/or teacher. Mentoring is primarily a learner-focused relationship that provides protégés both challenges and substantial support for their emotional, technical, and informational development. The relationship is primarily, though not exclusively, focused on professional development and career advancement and often involves an influential person's significant help in advancing a protégé's professional goals. A hopeful outcome of the relationship is one of both professional and organizational development.

The origin of the word "mentoring" has been traced back to Greek mythology, when King Odysseus, or Ulysses in Latin, entrusted his son,

> ### EXERCISE
>
> Recall all of the people in your life who helped you learn something important. List each and note what you learned from them. Include people in your family and personal life as well as those in your career.

Telemachus, to the goddess Athena, who had taken the form of an old friend of Odysseus' whose name was Mentor. Mentor—the goddess Athena in disguise—embodied both the male and female personas, and she, "in this androgyny, integrated both traditional feminine and traditional masculine qualities—nurturing, supportive, and protective as well as aggressive, assertive and risk taking."[1] In the role of Mentor, Athena acted as the counselor (Mentor) to Telemachus as he searched in vain for his father, who had by then gone off to the Trojan Wars.

However, the first actual recorded modern usage of the term "mentor" is in a 1699 volume[2] about Telemachus, in which the lead character is that of Mentor, and the term had morphed into the action verb of "mentoring." The action of mentoring, in its simplest form, is one-on-one encouragement, advice, or befriending for both the receiver and the provider. Historically this activity was primarily an informal one, voluntarily activated by self-selection and mutually agreed on by both participants. Only in recent decades has the process become a more formally recognized, institutionally supported strategy, viewed as a collaborative effort between and among individuals in organizations. The process promotes a caring and sharing atmosphere aimed at either enhancing personnel development within an organization or developing a career for those with advancement potential.

Informal and Formal Mentoring

Although informal mentoring, which develops spontaneously without formal assignment, has existed in many types of organizations for some time, more formal mentoring efforts have been occurring only in the past couple of decades. During this time the importance of mentoring has been recognized and appreciated in information services organizations and associations, as is evident with ongoing and new mentoring development programs in information services organizations. Previous to this, most aspects of what is now recognized as mentoring were almost entirely serendipitous.

Formalized mentoring has now developed to a point where positive links are being recognized through the successful careers of individuals who benefited from being mentored and from the associated mentoring activities committed by more experienced colleagues. The basic strategy is one of implementing mentoring activities through a formalized program in which both the explicit attributes of a mentor, including expertise, skills, and proficiencies, and his or her more intangible attributes, including a positive attitude and perspective toward the systematic development of a protégé, can be captured in a career development process within an organization to achieve or maintain success.

In such a three-pronged approach, it becomes a win-win situation for the individual, the mentor, and the organization: the protégé benefits from the expertise of an experienced, committed mentor and achieves job satisfaction; the mentor benefits from the success that comes to the protégé as well as the enhancement of his or her own reputation as an expert and leader; and the organization benefits from the enhanced performance that leads to success and extends the reputation of the information services organization, while fostering an attitude of cooperation.

In most instances—whether the process is a formal organizational group mentoring program in which senior staff mentor junior staff or a more informal mentoring process between two people who share mutual interests—the basic reasons and the many benefits of the mentoring process are similar. It is a process in which everyone involved learns. It is recognition of the mentor's expertise and interpersonal skills. It is also an efficient and effective way of developing a junior colleague's knowledge and abilities to demonstrate deeper on-the-job proficiencies. Such a successful relationship reflects well on both the person being mentored and the mentor who gains respect and recognition as a professional role model.

Formal mentoring programs should be designed primarily as a rewarding process. For individuals committed to learning collaboratively or simply sharing and confirming ideas, getting involved in mentoring offers a great opportunity.

In successful, evolving library and information services organizations, staff development is becoming a primary factor for institutional success. Such future-oriented organizations seek meaningful ways for continued organizational development through their most important resource—their staff. One of these ways is the mentoring process. They use mentoring programs to improve morale, develop complementary teams, boost operational learning, build retention rates of valuable staff, provide career development, and improve leadership development.

Previous to the relatively recent development of formal mentoring activities in libraries and other information services organizations, the most prevalent method for individual professional development was to foster "role models," persons to be emulated and whose advice was sought. This type of mentoring consisted primarily of leading by example, often without either a formal structure or a specific commitment, when a member of an organization demonstrated traits and abilities that promoted the view of a "role model." Mentoring is not about the professional gain of a mentor at the expense of a protégé, nor is it a "one model fits all" approach. It is not even about a protégé seeking someone to direct his or her professional development. Rather, it is the interaction of colleagues for the betterment of the organization and the staff. At present a mentor is most often envisioned as a person who possesses certain desirable traits, characteristics, or talents. Terms used to describe these characteristics include "role model," "teacher," "guide," and "sage." A person earns these descriptors through his or her abilities to promote the development of other individuals in a compassionate way.

There are two basic "types" of mentoring, one that develops informally as a natural part of personnel development and one that develops from a more formal, planned process. The first type can be observed in everyday work situations where it appears to develop naturally among colleagues. It comes through everyday activities when colleagues become friends or through informal counseling and teaching related to organizational development. It takes place in many organizations, often when a manager identifies a developing talent. However, one negative aspect of informal mentoring, with the immediate supervisor being the mentor, is the impression of preferential treatment, the manager being perceived as "playing favorites" or even subordinating team needs to individual ones. The second and perhaps more important scenario occurs more formally through a structured program in which the person being mentored and the mentor are brought together specifically.

In the past, the stereotypical view of mentoring was that it was an exclusively male-dominated activity, most often a career-driven relationship, mutually beneficial for both the mentor—an experienced, powerful male—and a younger, less experienced "mentee," also male. It was a traditional "admixture of good father and good friend, a transitional figure who invites and welcomes a young man into the adult world."[3] Fortunately, this relationship is no longer a primary—and certainly not "the" singular—activity. Furthermore, the process is no longer viewed as simply a male-dominated "power trip" activity.

Both the concept and most activities previously related to mentoring have changed and consequently been implemented into more formal, voluntary, self-selected, mutually agreeable, multicultural, and dual gender relationships. Many of today's information services organizations have increasingly institutionalized the traditional concept, while introducing some innovative approaches to the give-and-take activities involved in mentoring. One primary reason is the recognition that, in order to survive and flourish, dynamic organizations need to implement more formalized efforts to develop the next generation of leaders. In such an ensuing mentoring culture, learning organizations are being encouraged in their collective effort to develop meaningful ways to connect personnel, for both institutional and personal benefit, which can lead to improving morale as well as enhancing work performance. An analytical acronym, employing the action terms applicable to the process, is **M**odel, **E**mpathize, **N**urture, **T**each, **O**rganize, **R**espond.

Mentoring is rapidly becoming one of the most efficient and effective ways of improving workplace performance. In most cases where formal mentoring has been introduced and implemented within an organization, the process is considered a powerful force, helping to shape the future of those organizations through intentional learning programs that enlighten both participants in a process. This effort has encouraged the mentor–protégé relationship to move from an abstract level to a more pragmatic one in which formally established educational programs are introduced and implemented. In this kind of activity, both the mentor and the protégé share a learning responsibility through the process of first setting and then implementing clearly defined goals for the process's success.

Somewhat contrarily the viewpoint also exists that less formalized mentorship relationships can improve both psychological and career initiatives, thereby suggesting that formally assigned or developed mentorship may sometimes result in less identification, less relational comfort, less motivation for mentoring, and ultimately less communication and interaction than the more informal ones.[4] Whether the two approaches are complementary or contrary remains a discussion point.

The development of "networks of mentors" has become more prevalent in today's information services organizations. Sometimes this is based on the protégé's career aspirations. The network of mentors allows protégés to take advantage of various professionals' expertise as they develop their aspiring careers.

Although mentoring and coaching are similar and often confused with each other, they are not the same. Coaching is a teaching "technique" that involves formally observing workers and then providing them with feedback to enhance their performance. The primary commonality between a mentor and a coach is that they use similar sets of techniques and skills, primarily communication and other interpersonal skills, to help colleagues. Therefore, in many situations, effective mentors do use coaching skills. However, a mentor, and those he or she mentors, are usually in the same organization, whereas coaches often are external experts brought in to teach certain important approaches and techniques to advance the organization's mission.

Functions of Mentoring

Mentors, to be successful role models, must be committed to their protégés' development. They provide a variety of directions and actions necessary for the successful transformation of the protégés. Mentors encourage protégés to think beyond current work assignments and professional capabilities toward future responsibilities and capabilities.

Organizations develop formal mentoring programs to help individuals develop skills, both technical and social, primarily to enhance personal career development. Formal programs have specific purposes, goals, and expected outcomes. In some programs, individual recipients are paired with seasoned mentors to aid in advancing careers, developing management skills, and identifying and overcoming deficiencies. In other programs, where goals and objectives are less structured, arrangements are made on a more informal basis where mentoring develops naturally, without a formal structure. Goals and objectives are more informal, and the act of mentoring just happens. So, it can be easily observed that there are several types and levels of mentoring. Depending on the situation, one might need some structured instruction in a work environment with a less formal nurturing relationship over a period of time—this correlates with the original mentoring example—or a more formal, structured program of mentoring.

Both the mentor and the protégé should clearly understand, at the very outset, the purpose and expected outcomes of the mentoring relationship. They should agree on the following factors at the beginning:

> **QUICK TIP**
>
> Some traps mentors should avoid:
> - "I know what is best."
> - "I can help you get ahead."
> - "You need me to be successful."
> - Reserving the difficult issues or areas for coaching.

1. **Purpose**: why you are together and what is expected of the relationship
2. **Communication**: preferred methods of keeping in tough, i.e., in person, via telephone, text messaging, e-mail, mail, etc.
3. **Trust**: establishing confidence in the process and the relationship
4. **Process**: planning, building relationship/negotiating agreement, developing the protégé, maintaining momentum, and ending the formal mentoring part of the relationship
5. **Feedback**: positive and corrective feedback

Personnel development, of course, has long been an important part of most successful organizations. Developing personnel to achieve that success has, likewise, been a focus in most successful information services organizations. However, certain aspects of personnel development, primarily through mentoring, have only recently been added, as an action, not a tool, to transform organizations and enhance success. It is now more widely recognized that developing the next generation of leaders can no longer be left to chance. Formal mentoring activities are now supplementing, and in many cases replacing, the informal mentoring relationships that have existed in many organizations.

This developmental process has several functions: for the protégé it is a way to enhance on-the-job skills while at the same time developing intellectual capital. It both facilitates the protégé's entry into a formal work setting and hastens the organization's ability to achieve information services goals. Through the more formalized acceptance of a process, the protégé can observe and question, having the sounding board of a mentor familiar with the organization and the processes for individual success.

Organizational Mentoring

Mentoring is becoming a critical element in many of today's successful information services organizations, because they have recognized the intrinsic benefits of these programs. Formal programs have developed learning partnerships that foster improved morale, career development, and establishment of team-building processes, all of which lead to retention of good staff members. The primary role is development of the person being mentored through efforts of confidence building, self-awareness, and networking opportunities. This approach also benefits managers who are also mentors by distinguishing the differences between the role of manager and that of mentor, including empowering and supporting others.

Listening, as opposed to "telling," is a critical ingredient in the manager–mentor relationship to develop protégé professionals. This is a time when protégés are more attuned to their own strengths and weaknesses. An information services organization's mentoring program should have a structured time frame, with a pre-matched exercise for pairing of the mentor and protégé. This involves matching the interests, expertise, and interpersonal traits of both participants with their assigned responsibilities and with the potential future needs of the information services organization. Steps for developing a mentor–protégé program include the following:

1. Match the protégé with a mentor based on the mission of the organization, the goals of the protégé, and the expertise of the mentor.

2. Identify the expectations of the process and of both the mentor and the protégé, followed by a training session to discuss time

---

ARE YOU READY TO BE A MENTOR?
A SELF-ASSESSMENT

Think about the following questions, which should be followed by a positive "yes" before you assume a formal mentoring role:

1. Do I have the necessary experience to be a good mentor? If not, do I have the talent and drive to learn these capabilities?

2. Do I have the status, reputation, organizational experience, and basic capabilities that will permit me to develop and assume a positive mentoring role? Am I viewed as having the expertise and aptitude for intellectual engagement to be a good mentor?

3. Do I have leadership skills, such as those of networking and counseling, to develop good mentoring relationships?

4. Do I have the necessary knowledge of the current developments, including both managerial and the accelerating technological ones, required to generate a positive experience for a potential protégé?

5. Do I realistically have the time, patience, and energy, given my current workload, to assume the responsibilities necessary to be a successful mentor?

6. Conversely, what would I get out of such a mentoring relationship? Will I, personally and professionally, benefit from such a professional relationship?

7. Do I, upon self-examination, possess the knowledge and personal and organizational abilities required, and am I capable of instilling like ones in a protégé in order for him or her to grasp their importance for organizational development?

8. Am I a nonjudgmental person in my observations and comments about issues and potential resolutions that the protégé might identify in consequences that might develop?

9. How adept am I in providing useful, truthful input, feedback, and directions without being critical or arrogant? Do I have or am I capable of developing the interpersonal skills necessary to identify personal goals and values and discuss them openly, thereby providing desirable feedback?

10. Am I a good listener and communicator? Do I have the skills necessary to let a protégé discover, on his or her own, issues and suggest solutions to them?

11. Am I astute enough to recognize the degree of dependence or independence desirable at various stages of a mentoring relationship? Can I recognize the fine line between counseling and dictating?

12. Am I astute enough to recognize values and opinions without imposing my own?

13. Am I capable of recognizing the fine line between professional counseling and personal problem solving— the latter of which must be avoided in the work relationship?

frame, place(s) of instruction/consultation, venues for inter-action, and forms of evaluation of success, with recognition of disappointment, if any.

3. Construct and sign an agreement. Formal mentoring processes are regulated by signed agreements that serve as a guide or "contract" for activities development, with follow-up formal evaluative processes. It is a guide for both participants, outlining such directions as meeting times and places and important support activities, which can include professional meetings, local conferences on specific topics, etc., in the time allocated. The contract also addresses the developmental objectives, including measuring success in achieving the objectives as well as effectiveness of the mentor's activities.

4. Agree to maintain confidentiality between mentor and protégé.

5. End with a formal, written evaluation of the process when it has been completed.

Peer-to-Peer and Group Mentoring

Many information services organizations are now developing peer mentoring programs where new or inexperienced professionals are paired with either individuals or groups of staff members in like positions. The peer relationship is a forum for the mutual exchange of experiences and observations, which becomes a learning mode for participants. Such exchanges, it might be noted, provide a comforting sense of both equality and empathy that is sometimes perceived as lacking in the more formal approach. This type of semi-structured mentoring and sharing is often informal yet sanctioned by the organization because it is conducted within the context of the organization's needs and goals. In these cases the organization facilitates the activities by bringing together staff members who have a common need and interest with other staff who have experience and information to share.

As an example, group mentoring or multiple mentoring relationships include activities within the group as well as one-on-one mentoring activities with individuals rotating among several identified mentors. Such arrangements are developed to take advantage of a larger pool of identified mentors and to provide an expanded pool of mentors who can then:

1. create a wider network for the pool of identified protégés in the information services organization;

2. receive similar feedback from the same multiple sources, thereby experiencing a comparable organizational knowledge base;

3. bond as a network and move at a similar pace in knowledge development and responsibility development;

4. facilitate a greater mentoring culture within the organization; and

5. encourage protégés to continue developing after they become experienced mentors.

The greatest advantage of this group approach is that the sharing of processes and knowledge bases leads to speedier professional development in a supportive environment.

Therefore, because it is possible, and even likely, that the organization has more than one mentor–protégé process, an important secondary issue is evaluating a total program in relation to success for the organization. Achieving the institution's goals, retaining valuable staff, developing those with identified potential, and maintaining high morale within the organization are points to be considered.

Roles and Responsibilities of a Mentor

Mentoring is a beneficial way for a potential mentor to revive and further enhance skills and attitudes that may be laying dormant. To establish a successful relationship requires development of "trust" within the relationship, which is based on openness about needs and expectations. Openness occurs when those involved feel safe, not vulnerable, in revealing weaknesses as well as strengths. Trust is the basis of such collaboration, because everything else in the relationship is based on mutual trust.[5]

The process of establishing a mutually beneficial partnership allows one with expertise to provide appropriate and accurate guidance to an identified, usually through mutual acceptance, protégé with whom the mentor can explore issues, define approaches, introduce contact persons, and, perhaps, enhance his or her own reputation in the process. It also entails assisting in the development of skills and behavior of the individuals being mentored. A mentoring program can be developed in several ways, including one-on-one relationships, as well as peer group mentoring, and even electronic mentoring.

Several traits are important for the mentor to possess, the most significant being that of a teacher. This attribute is vital in the relationship, because the primary intent is to develop skills and improve performance. The teaching role requires identifying the core of information needed and the best way to transmit that knowledge. It entails using proper teaching methodology and developing a plan to instill a core of knowledge, responsibility, and action. It requires stepping back and analyzing the kinds of information needed and the most appropriate approach to imparting it to the protégé. This can be through teaching by example, by observation, and by repetition.

An equally important trait is that of listener, identifying concerns and allaying them through examples of one's own experiences or observations. Expressions of empathy tend to relax a superior–subordinate relationship and encourage openness between the two.

It is a primary responsibility of the mentor to listen, empathize, and caution and give criticism only when appropriate. The mentor must admit his or her own ignorance and mistakes when they occur, recognizing that mentors are not perfect and can be learners as well. Values identification is another important aspect of the mentoring process through which personal values are identified and ultimately demonstrated.

A mentor's role in the mentor–protégé relationship also includes the following:

1. Communicating by setting an interactive environment, conducive to encouragement and sharing information

2. Advising on career-related issues and developmental approaches in reaching career goals, identifying and encouraging skills development and recommending programs and activities advantageous to career development

3. Representing the protégé's activities and ideas within promotion opportunities

4. Promoting the protégé's abilities to a wider audience through identification of developing talents of the protégé

5. Encouraging the protégé in both educational and other knowledge-related pursuits

Before assuming the responsibilities of a mentor, one should consider one's own attributes and responsibilities. Some of the expectations of a mentor include the following:

1. Mentors will be knowledgeable about their organization and its wider environment and be willing to share in a give and take relationship.

2. Mentors will be perceived in the organization as role models, with good interpersonal skills.

3. Mentors will be dedicated to the learning and development of others.

4. Mentors will have the ability and determination to motivate others.

5. Mentors will always maintain confidentiality.

Key Factors for a Successful Mentor–Protégé Relationship

Key factors that determine the success of a mentoring program include:

- **commitment** by all involved;
- **clarity** regarding purpose, desired outcomes, defined target group, and resources available for implementation; and

- **communication** that is open so that everyone knows about the program and its goals.

A mentor assists in the development of a protégé rather than assesses his or her performance. The mentor is an adviser, a consultant, a role model, and, often, a colleague. In a mentoring relationship, the protégé seeks to identify problems, share issues, and ask for advice from mentors, who do not evaluate them. However, it is primarily the responsibility of the mentor to set goals and establish objectives, and this should be done and clearly stated during the first session of a formal mentoring relationship. Setting goals is critical. They give the relationship a distinct purpose and help both participants to organize and articulate their expectations. Well-defined goals guide the work to be done together and provide a focus.

The mentor not only sets goals but also demonstrates the need for the protégé to set goals. The mentor helps the protégé develop the necessary skills to effectively establish and efficiently pursue appropriate goals. Goals will include points of structure for the program, for instance, where, when, and how often the mentor and protégé should meet and what communication tools (in-person conversations, written progress reports, telephone, e-mail) would be helpful in the relationship (they will vary from one situation to another).

The schedule for sessions should remain flexible, depending on other responsibilities. Accessibility is an important factor in the relationship, as well as open communication. Some mechanism for feedback is important, because there needs to be feedback on the expectations of the process and satisfaction with the developing outcomes. Having identified periods for feedback is important so that tensions over performance or advice do not hinder the formal relationship. These times also serve as evaluation points in the scheduled process.

The protégé learns best through a systematic approach developed through meaningful assignments.[6] A written plan is the best way of ensuring progress. The important initial steps in the relationship, demonstrated through the mentor's knowledge and professional integrity, can develop into a quality of inspiration, of setting an example and challenging the protégé to be all he or she can be.

There are several variations of the traditional face-to-face, one-on-one approach, some of which were briefly mentioned earlier:

1. Group mentoring, as discussed earlier in this chapter, involves more than one mentor for a protégé, thereby, through this team mentoring approach, taking advantage of the unique skills of many individuals who share their knowledge and expertise.

2. Group-circle mentoring involves more than one protégé per mentor who possesses specific expertise. A number of people participate in a learning group setting, benefiting from the experience and expertise of a mentor or mentors. This approach also helps resolve the organizational issue of wanting to mentor many people when there are not enough qualified mentors to make one-to-one mentoring matches or when it is desirable to take advantage of the specific knowledge base of several experts.

Did You Know?
Individuals who are mentored tend to gain these benefits:

- Understanding of the political context and culture of the organization
- Advancement toward personal mastery
- Stronger commitment to personal learning and development
- More confidence in themselves and their ability to achieve high performance
- Appreciation of networking and developing a broader set of professional relationships
- A more expansive perspective on their career possibilities

Such group mentoring also avoids the perception of favoritism that can result when there are limited numbers of mentors and many potential protégés.

3. Some information services organizations will enlist professionally trained mentors and coaches to address specific issues.

4. Peer group mentoring sometimes develops, formally or informally, in information services organizations when there is an identified need to develop a certain knowledge base to support the organizational goals. This is usually a self-organized and managed arrangement to take advantage of group members' expertise. Like group mentoring, peer group mentoring can encourage diversity in thinking, practices, perspectives, interactions, and understanding to promote organizational development.

5. E-mentoring is now developing where a mentoring relationship is established primarily or exclusively online. Tele-mentoring programs use the Internet for e-mailing and other forms of electronic communication. These programs provide opportunities for mentoring relationships that were previously restricted by geographical boundaries.

6. Reverse mentoring sometimes occurs to aid more senior members of an organization in learning, through the knowledge of younger professionals, particularly in the field of advanced information technology, computing, and Internet communications.

Libraries and other information services organizations use formal mentoring for several reasons. These include, among others, indoctrinating new employees into the organizational culture and facilitating both professional and personal development of organizational members and, later, their career development. Just as important, formal mentoring is often introduced in organizations to develop colleagues who have previously been hampered by barriers related to being women or members of a minority group.

Criteria for establishing a successful mentoring relationship of course include developing mutual trust and respect by both parties. Although in some situations the chemistry may not be immediately in place, it can be built over time. The primary factor is being able to trust that it can be developed within a reasonable period. This is most likely to occur if the mentor is committed to the relationship.

The mentor, being a seasoned member of the organization, already possesses desirable knowledge—of the organization and its relationship to a greater community—as well as an understanding of the organization's goals and objectives, policies and procedures, and functions. Besides a sound understanding of the organization itself, a good mentor is expected to possess certain characteristics, including good communication and interpersonal skills and a reasonable personal network of colleagues who can be tapped for certain knowledge that can be helpful in successfully achieving the goals of the mentoring project.

IMPLEMENTING AN EFFECTIVE MENTORING PROGRAM: GUIDELINES FOR MENTORS AND PROTÉGÉS

Mentors help protégés think beyond their current roles and perceived capabilities. At various times mentors will have the roles of sponsor, counselor, coach, positive role model, developer of competencies and talent, promoter of professional activities and engagement, sounding board, confidant, challenger, political advisor, opener of doors, developer of careers, and/or teacher. It is helpful to keep each of these roles in mind and to envision ways in which each might be carried out.

Following are some suggestions for success in the mentoring relationship:

Attributes for the Mentor

- Develop a relaxed atmosphere, and be forthcoming as yourself in interactions with a protégé.
- Demonstrate a caring, concerned demeanor, and convey empathy.
- Be alert in observing behavior, and be aware of nonverbal clues.
- Be available for consultation on a regular, scheduled basis and when otherwise needed.
- Develop a problem-solving approach by clarifying issues or situations and identifying and addressing the options available.
- Be an active listener in conversations with protégés. Seek to offer advice, new perspectives, suggestions, and encouragement as appropriate.
- Maintain confidentiality at all times.
- Offer options, ask effective questions, and provide constructive feedback and alternative approaches where applicable and when necessary.

Skills for the Mentor

- Observing behavior and nonverbal cues as they develop
- Demonstrating concern for feelings and attention to behavior
- Conveying empathy to enforce trust
- Solving problems, performing situational analyses, and providing feedback and suggestions for options
- Suggesting and evaluating career options with protégés and recommending strategies for developing a successful direction
- Asking pertinent questions

Skills for Protégés

- Developing an eagerness for learning
- Maintaining openness in the relationship
- Recognizing risk-taking as an important developmental activity
- Identifying successes and failures in the learning process and being open to discussing them with the mentor
- Effectively receiving and evaluating constructive feedback
- Committing to one's own learning and development

Mentoring Roles, Responsibilities, and Competencies

Did You Know?
E.M. Forster once said, "One person with passion is better than forty people merely interested." One of the greatest gifts mentors can give is passion—to share their passion and to stimulate passion in those they mentor.

Several common roles that mentors perform can be easily identified and include the following:

1. Mentors advise and counsel by sharing experiences and insights and offering recommendations while listening to the protégé's own ideas and potential plans. The purpose is to work with the protégé in setting realistic career goals and pursuing professional interests based on a development plan.

2. Mentors coach by examining the protégé's background and experiences, identifying strengths and weaknesses, suggesting new skills, and providing feedback on resulting outcomes (coaching is discussed in detail in Chapter 6).

3. Mentors motivate and encourage protégés to consider advancing professionally by assuming more responsibilities at an appropriate time in their development.

4. Mentors tutor and teach protégés not only by adopting a how-to-do-it approach but also by sharing specific facts and other information acquired through their own experiences and responsibilities within an organization.

5. Mentors are role models, teaching by example as well as through the performance of their own organizational roles and responsibilities. Role models demonstrate values, ethics, and exemplary professional practice, and experience has shown that protégés often imitate their mentors.

6. Mentors support protégés in their organizational assignments, and they facilitate access to further educational opportunities, professional contacts, and assignments.

7. As trusted professionals, with confidentiality and mutual respect in place, mentors counsel protégés in professional matters and work development and challenge them as confidants through open discussions of private matters and problems.

8. Mentors create a supportive network by promoting, identifying, and seeking professional activities, organizations, programs, and engagements applicable to the protégés' career development.

9. Mentors help protégés develop competencies, values, attitudes, and talents that are aligned with the strategic thinking and planning of the information services organization.

10. Mentors teach developmental skills and offer help and encouragement to develop the knowledge base required to successfully perform obligations by, among other things, interpreting policies and procedures.

11. Mentors coach protégés to develop career goals (as described in Chapter 6).

Think About It
What is your passion in your work and professional life today?

Notes

1. Jeruchim, Joan, and Pat Shapiro. 1992. *Women, Mentors, and Success.* New York: Fawcett Columbine, p. 24.
2. Fénelon, François de Salignac de la Motte. 1699. *Les Aventures de Telemaque.*
3. Levinson, Daniel J., et al. 1978. *The Seasons of a Man's Life.* New York: Ballantine, p. 333.
4. Kram, K.E. 1985. *Mentoring at Work: Developmental Relationships in Organizational Life.* Glenview, IL: Scott Foresman.
5. Ensher, Ellen A., and Susan E. Murphy. 2005. *Power Mentoring: How Successful Mentors and Protégés Get the Most Out of Their Relationships.* San Francisco: Jossey-Bass, pp. 142–152.
6. Ambrose, Larry. 1996. *A Mentor's Companion.* Chicago: Perrone-Ambrose.

Succession Planning and Development

Even if you're on the right track, you'll get run over if you just sit there.

— Will Rogers

Succession Planning Defined

Today the importance of succession planning cannot be ignored in an information services organization's human resources system. Succession planning involves recruitment, training, retention, and performance management, important factors that enhance an organization's future human resources. Several points can distinguish it from the more traditional human resources training processes. Primarily it:

1. focuses on leadership and management in critical positions within the information services organization to ensure a continuity of leadership;

2. is a total organizational process to identify and develop talents of individuals rather than just focusing on current competencies of staff members;

3. identifies and develops not just one person but perhaps several with potential leadership abilities for elevation when applicable positions become available;

4. focuses on creating and developing a pool of staff with leadership potential; and

5. facilitates the inevitable organizational leadership transition.

Succession planning is a systematic process to maintain leadership continuity in key positions while retaining and developing the knowledge and experience of personnel to ensure the organization's future success. Succession planning is about matching emerging or identified talents with predicted leadership roles, but not necessarily specific positions. The activities developed for this process are intended to prepare any

IN THIS CHAPTER:

✔ Succession Planning Defined

✔ Some Strategies and Approaches

✔ The Leader's Role

✔ Steps in Succession Planning

✔ Assessing Competencies

✔ Key Criteria for an Effective Program

promising individual for leadership roles but does not guarantee future promotions.

There are two nomenclatures to describe this activity in today's libraries: "succession planning" and "succession management." As information services organizations begin to plan for succession from the managers of today to those of the future, the characteristics and strengths of these new managers also must be taken into consideration. Management and leadership skills are both an art and a set of skills, and many aspects can be taught and learned through observation and practice.

For the purpose of this discussion, the concepts of planning and management are combined, recognizing that there are differences; they are often viewed as complementary, with one enhancing the other. Succession planning is not simply about one specific job. It should be accepted that "succession planning is the culmination of effective management development."[1] Succession planning is designed to ensure the continued effective performance of an organization's staff by making provision for the development and replacement of key persons over time. It is an effort to identify, assess, develop, and retain talented colleagues at every level—management, professional, and technical—within the information services organization. It helps organizations develop a diverse workforce as it identifies and monitors the talent pool in order to match future needs of the organization with the strengths of in-house talent. It is a key strategy for addressing human resources needs and encourages individual advancement within the information services organization. It also encourages:

1. acquiring insight into the information services organization's workforce through a focus on each individual's background, performance, expertise, and career aspirations;

2. identifying what here-to-fore might have been undiscovered talents;

3. building on existing talents within the organization while also identifying potential weaknesses—in an effort to groom employees for more challenging positions; and

4. facilitating the identification of qualified persons to fill potential leadership gaps.

To put it simply, it is planning for future leaders in information services.

The cliché about having the right person in the right place at the right time for the right reason sums up the objective of succession management. A good succession planning system is developmentally oriented rather than simply replacement oriented. Therefore, the process can be described as a strategic, systematic, deliberate activity developed to ensure an organization's successful future through the employment of the right people, at the right time, in the right positions. This challenge involves not only the identification of internal candidates in a concerted effort to develop a good personnel infrastructure within the organization but also an effective recruitment program to identify qualified external candidates for positions in the information services organization. Traditionally, succession planning in information services organizations has been more of what might be described as replacement planning. The relatively new, more formalized succession planning process takes the traditional replacement strategy an important step forward toward being a methodical process of forecasting workforce needs and developing promotional strategies to meet those needs. One side benefit is that the manager's role is enhanced through the process of identifying potential leaders and recommending staff for promotion.

To achieve the objectives, a formalized plan is needed to facilitate the succession of current key staff. An assessment of the current workforce is a critical first step in this systematic effort to identify individuals with potential, an action intended to help continue the transformation of an organization's vision into reality. With the goal of ensuring a talented future workforce, the organization's personnel needs are first identified and then a strategic personnel development plan is developed to meet those needs. In some forward-looking information services organizations, additional "leadership goals are being met through the organization's strategic-planning efforts that include the identification of critical positions requiring priority attention."[2] This aligns the human resources development aspects of the plan with the strategic directions of the information services organization itself.

Think About It
Identify what you and your organization are doing to promote succession planning. What additional steps can you take?

Some Strategies and Approaches

Because leadership development is the goal, a plan is needed to address the succession of current key personnel while at the same time developing the knowledge base of future leaders. This is not a simple replacement strategy but rather an attempt to forecast the future workforce needs and then continuously pursuing strategies to meet those needs. The strategies must incorporate both staff training and leadership development. This naturally ties into the strategic planning exercise performed by most forward-looking institutions to identify their vision, mission, and values.[3] This connection to the strategic planning process ensures that the process is mission driven and reflects the identified priorities of the information services organization.

Succession planning provides several benefits. Primarily, it is a useful, even strategic, training tool with which to improve retention and prepare staff for leadership roles. A secondary, possibly as important, advantage is that it serves as a morale booster, promoting staff satisfaction. Additionally, it encourages greater commitment to organizational goals, thereby improving the organization's image in the greater workplace, whether academic, public school, or special information services.

Within the organization, one primary issue in succession planning is identifying potential candidates without demoralizing those not chosen. One criterion is having the greatest potential, a quality easily identified by management and human resources development personnel. The more traditional performance review process can also be used to identify potential candidates. However, a disadvantage of this method is that those not given an opportunity may become disenchanted. A third method, which is seldom used, is one of self-selection whereby those who perceive their leadership talents apply for an announced leadership process. Once the candidates are identified, they can begin preparing themselves for future leadership by using some of these methods:

1. Attend leadership training programs. There are many such programs, some of which are designed specifically for librarians and others that more generically focus on skills and competencies.

2. Focus on personal development. Identify specific skills and areas for growth and attend a training program or perform other activities to address them.

3. Pursue specific work experiences, including taking on additional responsibilities in current positions, to try new skills that foster intellectual growth, thereby enhancing confidence and competence.

4. Pursue hands-on opportunities that involve leadership activities, such as supervisory responsibilities, with constructive feedback, to develop desired skills and knowledge bases.

5. Rotate jobs to test different skills and increase individual as well as organizational knowledge.

6. Assume responsibilities that encourage the development of new competencies not normally a part of the individual's current responsibilities.

7. Shadow leaders who are scheduled for retirement as a valuable learning exercise.

The most effective way of addressing succession management is to institute a continuous, somewhat simple process of identifying future leaders. A basic four-step process involves identifying the competencies needed, assessing individual capabilities, recruiting additional talents, and coaching individuals in goal-setting efforts to meet organizational needs. This requires setting up a routine process of identifying future leaders. Rothwell[4] devised a useful strategy to assist organizations in integrating succession planning into human resources development. It is a basic core set of leadership and succession management competencies:

1. Examine existing human resources programs, such as selection, training, compensation, and benefits, in light of succession planning needs.

2. Ensure managers give specific consideration to the long-term retention and development of high-potential employees.

3. Identify human resources practices that could encourage or that currently discourage effective succession planning.

4. Identify any disincentives that may exist that dissuade employees from wanting to accept promotions or leadership roles.

It is now commonly recognized that leadership is a quality that can be developed and that leaders do not operate in isolation. As information services institutions become more complex, it becomes vital to expose more individuals to opportunities for learning leadership skills. One preliminary, yet primary, task of succession planning is to outline a sequence of personnel moves so that candidates for key positions can be identified in advance of the actual need. This process of leadership capital development both encourages and accommodates current and future growth to occur without further interruption. Sometimes the issue of leadership development and succession planning is identified in an organization's periodic strategic plan. If future leadership needs are systematically identified, in this plan or in a separate one, an organization can more easily assess what competencies will be needed by employees in key leadership positions.

Throughout this book we describe key points regarding leadership needs and development, including coaching, mentoring, and team building. But leadership development itself consists of two intertwined components: the skills that need to be learned as well as the important

GUIDELINES FOR SUCCESSION PLANNING

1. Assess the library's future information services needs.

A strategic plan identifies current and future priorities that are the essence of building a succession plan. Develop strategies for meeting those needs.

2. Identify positions where staff members or potential employees require additional knowledge or training.

Critical positions are those that are essential to organizational success; assess the current workforce situation. Persons in critical positions must be capable of advancing to a higher position of responsibility or technical proficiency.

3. Identify competencies.

Revise job descriptions and make a commitment to continuously update them to reflect the current workplace.

4. Select training and development activities.

Identify and promote the variety of resources available to close the knowledge and abilities gaps and thereby build additional competencies.

5. Conduct management training.

Managers and other knowledgeable experts should participate in training focused on augmenting the skills and expanding the knowledge bases that employees must have to advance.

6. Implement development strategies and tactics.

Managers should determine when different strategies are needed, before they are implemented, and communicate them to employees.

7. Monitor and evaluate.

Once managers have implemented their succession plans, they should monitor progress, evaluate the implementation, and revise their plans as needed.

personal component. Combined, these complement the basic aptitude and desire to lead. However, it is obvious that additional training and greater team development is needed to accomplish a smooth transition into new responsibilities and new positions without interruption of ongoing workflow and services.

Although succession planning is becoming a more prevalent part of strategic planning in many forward-thinking information services organizations, at present it too often occurs only "just in time" rather than "just in case." It sometimes happens when an important management vacancy occurs and there has been no serious prior consideration of the consequences. In a desirable scenario, however, the process is strategic rather than reactive. This is because few events have such an impact on an information services organization as the departure of key personnel, particularly identified leaders in the organization. Yet such a void will likely have a lasting impact on the inner workings of the information services organization, and it can potentially affect external perceptions of not only the departing incumbent's effectiveness but also the organization as it is viewed by colleagues in other information services organizations.

Perhaps the greatest need for succession planning is contained in a primary challenge to the profession, a profession that is adjusting to the development of technological innovations for information services. That challenge is in the graying of the profession. With a substantial number of senior staff—including directors, deans and head librarians, as well as department heads—reaching retirement age, the need to take a new look at the future of the profession is paramount. At the same time, this scenario also presents a unique opportunity to develop the next generation of information services leaders. This dual challenge is one of leadership development and succession planning. With adequate preparation for succession, identified staff members can seamlessly move into leadership challenges and facilitate new directions for information services.

The Leader's Role

One vital aspect of a leader's role is to make succession management and leadership development a top priority. This requires not only advocating succession planning but also becoming active in the primary responsibility of identifying and developing talent. A different perspective is needed, one that is different from the traditional view of replacement planning. It requires a calculated review of the pool of talented employees and recruitment efforts for potential employees and then development of a retention strategy so that those most clearly qualified are encouraged to remain. Such an effort also examines the reasons people might leave the organization and therefore requires adjustment of priorities to reflect retention goals.

The human factor in any organization is shaped by managerial actions and leadership. One of the greatest factors in organizational success is the motivation of employee performance and organizational effectiveness.

Think About It
Identify those with whom you work and want to be sure to retain. What will it take to do this?

The most important objective is to identify, motivate, and retain potential leaders through a series of training initiatives. This will lead to greater satisfaction with the work of the organization, thereby enhancing commitment to the organization and increasing the likelihood of achieving the organization's goals. The succession planning process does not have a finite approach and should be implemented with a realistic view of future challenges, not necessarily tied to the imminent departure of one who is currently in a leadership position. A planned succession policy should outline and follow the steps necessary to ensure an orderly transition that is beneficial for the organization.

Simply stated, a formal succession plan involves a process of first identifying and then preparing candidates, primarily those already in the information services organization, for what is likely to be a new leadership role for them. This involves developing a feedback system that informs individuals in the organization of how they are doing— identifying their positive leadership points while also identifying weaknesses that need to be corrected through programs already existing in the organization and through continuing education opportunities. These feedback opportunities may be developed as a formal program within the organization, such as an annual or six-month review process, at which time it is discussed whether employees are performing at optimal levels and whether they exhibit the kinds of abilities identified as important to leadership roles within the organization. Other feedback opportunities can be developed through a more informal, ongoing approach in addition to the normal performance review. Some of the training aspects may be important for everyone as they learn new skills and knowledge that are useful in current and future positions, while other aspects of training will be more individualized as aptitudes and talents are developed and organizationally recognized. In some organizations people are encouraged to "expand their capacity to create the results they truly desire, where new and expansive patterns of things are nurtured, where collective aspiration is set free, and where people are continually learning how to learn together."[5]

Steps in Succession Planning

A methodical approach to developing a program in succession planning entails, first of all, a commitment to prepare for inevitable leadership change. The ongoing process of systematically identifying, assessing, and developing talent to ensure leadership continuity for all key positions in an information organization is almost mandatory. The basic approach will include the following steps, after, of course, the information services organization commits to the concept and efforts involved in succession planning:

1. Analyze the demographics of the organization in terms of both structure and staffing. This process is a vital prerequisite to beginning any process for succession planning.

2. Identify "replacement needs" as a means of structuring a developmental program so that the necessary training and employee development can take place.

3. Plan and announce the profiles of ideal performers at all levels and for the future in order to meet the identified strategic objectives of the information services organization, with the objective of taking advantage of the identified intellectual capital.

4. Assess the talents that exist among current employees and their professional growth potential, thereby establishing the pool of eligible and promotable "leaders."

5. Compare the strengths and weaknesses of those identified with the above-mentioned profiles. Review and evaluate the work performances and competencies of these individuals and encourage them to develop competencies necessary for advancement.

6. Identify potential recruits for the organization, in addition to current employees, who might be eligible for leadership consideration within the organization.

7. Develop the potential leaders through a series of on-the-job and off-the-job training programs created to ensure a successful succession by narrowing any gaps between what expertise and talents they possess and what they would need.

8. Ascertain the success of the program. This evaluation is necessary to revise and enhance the program for better results.

Assessing Competencies

As mentioned, once an individual or a group of colleagues is recognized as being eligible for leadership opportunities and should be encouraged, it is necessary to in some way assess their levels of competency and then design a standard or unique development program to prepare each one for a higher level. To do this it is important first to articulate a set of skills desirable for performance in a leadership position. This also provides a measure for assessing the success of the preparation process.

Several standardized tests tap different leadership abilities and provide a reliable source of objective data to use to identify candidates' strengths and weaknesses. The Watson-Glaser Critical Thinking Appraisal[6] assesses various aspects of reasoning ability that align skills of problem solving and critical thinking to measure the capacity to understand the implications of specific aspects of a situation. It is a tool to evaluate analytical thinking, which is a key leadership aptitude. The Mayer and Salovey Model[7] measures the quality of interactions with others and the abilities to diagnose and address interpersonal difficulties that might limit consideration. The Leadership Competency Model,[8] developed at Central Michigan University, and the 360° Leadership Competencies Self Assessment[9] are also helpful testing tools. Such standardized tests aid in assessing the leadership strengths of prospective leaders and candidates for succession.

EXERCISES

1. Take a leadership competency test to assess your strengths and weaknesses as a leader. One example is on Central Michigan University's website (available at **www.chsbs.cmich.edu/leader_model/ Default.htm**).

2. Take the self-assessment test available on the same website (at **www .chsbs.cmich.edu/leader_model/longassmt_p1.asp**).

Key Criteria for an Effective Program

A number of criteria are important to keep in mind as an organization encourages and supports staff members and provides opportunities to pursue and learn from new challenges:

1. Managerial leaders should believe and recognize that there is a potential for all people to contribute beyond their current performance levels. In this regard, managers should not only expect staff to grow and develop but also present opportunities for this to occur.

2. Organizations need to have a clear and aspirational vision for the future. This vision will help inspire all staff members to contribute their best performance.

3. Organizations should use a systematic approach to identify and nurture talent.

4. Career paths, rather than career ladders, are available and should be recognized and implemented.

5. In every organization there is a diverse workforce, and this diversity should be recognized and valued.

6. It is necessary that information flow openly throughout the organization.

7. Staff, individually and collectively, are recognized and appreciated for their achievements and contributions.

8. Learning and development plans help spell out performance goals and identify areas for competency development.

9. Staff members expect and deserve regular, specific, and timely feedback on their performance. Managerial leaders should provide needed and positive reinforcement on an ongoing basis.

10. There is an explicit commitment to a broad and inclusive approach to succession management.

11. Senior leadership continually reaffirms its commitment to staff development and to the succession management program.

Notes

1. Cheloha, Randall S. 1999. "Hallmarks of Effective Succession Planning." *MMC Viewpoint Magazine* 2: 3.

2. Stueart, Robert D., and Barbara B. Moran. 2006. *Library and Information Center Management*, 7th ed. Westport, CT: Libraries Unlimited, p. 268.

3. Stueart and Moran, *Library and Information Center Management*, pp. 93–117.

4. Rothwell, William J. 2005. *Effective Succession Planning: Ensuring Leadership Continuity and Building Talent from Within*, 3rd ed. New York: AMACOM.

5. Senge, Peter M. 1990. *The Fifth Discipline: The Art and Practice of the Learning Organization*. New York: Doubleday, p. 3.

6. Pearson's Talent Assessment Group. 2008. *Watson-Glaser Critical Assessment*. Upper Saddle River, NJ: Pearson Education.

7. Salovey, Peter, Marc A. Brackett, and John D. Mayer. 2004. *Emotional Intelligence: Key Readings on the Mayer and Salovey Model*. Port Chester, NY: Dude Publishing/National Professional Resources.

8. "Leadership Competency Model." Mount Pleasant: Central Michigan University. Available: www.chsbs.cmich.edu/leader_model/model.htm (accessed February 11, 2010).

9. "360° Leadership Competencies Self Assessment." San Diego: Haines Centre Assessments. Available: www.hainescentre.com/pdfs/newsletter/ildr _sel_web.pdf (accessed February 11, 2010).

A Brief Afterword: Bringing It All Together

The greatest good you can do for another is not just to share your riches but to reveal to him his own.

— Benjamin Disraeli

The need for leadership development in information services organizations is obvious. It involves not only those persons in positions of making decisions and promoting action but also those identified as having the potential to be leaders. To encourage such potential requires organizational support for personnel development. Perhaps one of the first questions that come to mind when thinking about leadership development is the simple one: "Why and how should one become a mentor, or a coach, or even a team builder?" In the not too distant past many colleagues reached their management positions and achieved their pinnacles of management success without such specific organizational support but rather through hard work and some amount of luck.

But the projected future is no longer what it used to be. It is becoming evident that a different leadership effort is required, one that draws on the best intellectual, technical, and moral resources an organization has or can acquire. It requires staff who are thoughtful, well informed, active, and creative. Upon reflection, many managers can identify some support that enabled them in their journey up the success ladder. However, most of that support was informal, not specifically programmatic. It was serendipitous, not a planned cycle of activities. Many can recall the encouragement of mentors. Those rare opportunities were through informal arrangements to sit at the feet of a sage to "learn the ropes." The great mentors or coaches were not likely to have been identified by such a distinguished title. Fortunately, that "road less traveled" has now become a more organized, more focused, more rewarding, and more exciting "superhighway." Many information services colleagues now benefit from recent developments and opportunities for performance and personal development. The strategic reallocation of resources is becoming an essential starting point.

Extraordinary opportunities now facilitate the professional growth of potential leaders through an organized course of knowledge and wisdom sharing, accumulated and articulated by "sages and scholars" over a lifetime of experiences who are willing to impart their knowledge to "seekers." A logical beginning point requires considering how to maximize current leadership and staff development efforts in one's own information services organization. The prospect for development is an exciting two-way path involving knowledge seeking and action planning on the one hand and coaching, mentoring, and team building on the other. It involves both organizational initiative and individual commitment. Many are already benefiting from the changes, the new knowledge bases, the developing processes, and the eventual outcomes of these efforts. Others are seeking such opportunities. Such "value-added" strategic efforts are becoming necessary.

Skills enhancement and deliberate efforts toward knowledge acquisition are being encouraged because they create a win–win opportunity— explicating a mentor's or team leader's professional growth, thereby strengthening their leadership skills. This very activity enables leaders and potential leaders to improve their leadership skills and performance and set examples that can be emulated. Pursuing such attributes, with follow-up mentoring activities, will challenge potential leaders and effectively prepare their talented professionals and working colleagues in a "succession planning and retention activities" atmosphere. This is, perhaps, the most powerful and cost-effective program for recognizing talent and encouraging performance development.

Such a program includes mentoring, coaching, and team-building activities to foster the skills needed to influence and develop employee knowledge, abilities, and interests. Leadership success depends on developing these talents. An important side benefit of participating in the activities is developing self-reliance, self-confidence, and self-awareness. By promoting an environment of performance enhancement and development, an information services organization can take pride in its support and development of talented staff members. However, it is vital to view this process as performance enhancement rather than a remedial activity. The ensuing culture of enhancement will open up exciting new opportunities for both knowledge development and greater organizational success.

Index

Page numbers followed by the letter "f" indicate figures or sidebars.

About the Authors

Robert D. Stueart is Professor and Dean Emeritus of the Simmons College Graduate School of Library and Information Science, in Boston, where he was dean for almost 20 years. From 1994 through 1997, when he received the prestigious John F. Kennedy International Scholar Award, he served as Professor of Information Management in the School of Advanced Technologies and as Executive Director of the Center for Library and Information Resources at the Asian Institute of Technology in Bangkok, Thailand, where he developed both PhD and master's degree programs in information management. During his career, he also served on the faculties of the University of Denver, the University of Wales in the United Kingdom, and the University of Pittsburgh and on the senior administrative staffs of the libraries at both the University of Colorado and the Pennsylvania State University.

Dr. Stueart has received many honors, including the American Library Association's (ALA) highest award, that of Honorary Member; the Melvil Dewey Medal for "creative professional achievement"; and the Beta Phi Mu award for "service to education nationally and internationally," all presented by the ALA. In 1994, he was presented the Humphrey/OCLC Forrest Press International Award for "significant contributions to international librarianship." He has received outstanding alumni awards from all three of his degree-granting universities and an honorary PhD for his "international information services leadership" from Khon Kaen University in Thailand.

Professor Stueart has served in leadership roles in many professional organizations, including the executive board and the council of the ALA and the executive board of IFLA, the International Federation of Library Associations and Institutions. He has also served as president of three library associations: the Association for Library and Information Science Education; Beta Phi Mu, the international library science honor society; and the former Library Education Division of ALA. His co-authored textbook *Library and Information Center Management*, now in its seventh edition, has been called "a classic" by reviewing sources. He and Maureen Sullivan's first publication with Neal-Schuman was their 1991 manual *Performance Analysis and Appraisal*.

Maureen Sullivan is an independent organization development consultant whose practice focuses on the delivery of consulting and training services to libraries and other information services organizations. She has 30 years of experience as a consultant on organization development and effectiveness, strategic planning, leadership development, introducing and managing organizational change, organization and work redesign, establishment of staff development and learning programs for today's workplace, creating a work environment that supports diversity, revision of position classification and compensation systems, and the identification and development of competencies. Her experience includes 12 years as the human resources administrator in the libraries at the University of Maryland (1977–1980) and at Yale University (1983–1991).

Ms. Sullivan provides consulting and training services to a number and variety of library and information services organizations, including library networks and professional associations. Among the topics for which she has designed and offered workshops and learning institutes are leadership development, redesigning work, improving work relationships, managing stress, career planning, introducing the learning organization, process improvement, building teams, creating the collaborative organization, improving individual and organizational performance, generational synergy, cross-cultural communication, and project management.

Ms. Sullivan is the 2010 Association of College and Research Libraries' (ACRL) Academic/Research Librarian of the Year. The award, sponsored by YBP Library Services, recognizes an outstanding member of the library profession who has made a significant national or international contribution to academic/research librarianship and library development.

Ms. Sullivan is a past president (1998–1999) of the ACRL. During her term as president, she helped establish the ACRL/Harvard Leadership Institute in partnership with the Harvard Graduate School of Education. She is now a member of the faculty for this annual program. She was president of the Library Administration and Management Association for the 1988–1989 term. In 1999, she received the Elizabeth Futas Catalyst for Change Award from the ALA.

She is a Professor of Practice in the new PhD/Managerial Leadership in the Information Professions program at the Simmons College Graduate School of Library and Information Science.